Lawfare

This book examines one of the most emblematic cases of lawfare today: the criminal prosecution of former Brazilian President Lula. The authors argue that lawfare is not just a slogan or a game at the service of any one political ideology. Rather, it has to do with a complex, multifaceted phenomenon that should be carefully reflected upon in modern constitutional democracies, given that it is able to demolish majority rule and the rule of law. They contend it is the strategic use of the law with the purpose of delegitimizing, harming or annihilating an enemy. The literature specializing in the subject tends to alternate between analysis of only one aspect of the phenomenon or consists of extensive case studies. In order to fill this gap, this book revisits the subject and offers a sophisticated theoretical approach to lawfare, in an unprecedented combination of theory of war and theory of law.

The book will be of interest to students, researchers and policy makers working in the areas of public law, international law, procedural law, anthropology of law and sociology of law, as well as political science and international relations.

Cristiano Zanin is an Attorney and an expert in lawfare, transnational litigation, state investigations and bet-the-company litigation. He is a member of the Brazilian Lawyers Institute (IAB), the São Paulo Lawyers Association (AASP), and the International Bar Association (IBA). He is the co-founder of the Lawfare Institute. He is also coordinator of the legal defence of Luiz Inácio Lula da Silva, former President of Brazil, within "Operation Car Wash" and before the UN Human Rights Committee and other relevant proceedings pending before Brazilian courts.

Valeska Martins is an Attorney and an expert in lawfare, transnational litigation, bet-the-company and corporate law. She is a member of the International Bar Association (IBA) and coordinator of the legal defence of Luiz Inácio Lula da Silva, former President of Brazil, within "Operation Car Wash" and before the UN Human Rights Committee and other relevant proceedings pending before Brazilian courts.

Rafael Valim was Professor at the Pontifical Catholic University of São Paulo, Brazil, and is currently Simon Visiting Professor at the University of Manchester, UK, and Visiting Professor at Université Le Havre Normandie, France. He is one of Brazil's leading scholars of law and actively participates in Brazilian public debate. He has published a number of monographs and articles, which have been translated into several languages. He is also Editor-in-Chief of *Editora Contracorrente* and has held many visiting positions in France, Spain, Portugal, Italy, the UK and Latin America.

Lawfare
Waging War through Law

**Cristiano Zanin, Valeska Martins
and Rafael Valim**

**Translated by Colleen Boland
Revised by Linda Murur**

Routledge
Taylor & Francis Group

LONDON AND NEW YORK

First published 2022
by Routledge
2 Park Square, Milton Park, Abingdon, Oxon OX14 4RN

and by Routledge
605 Third Avenue, New York, NY 10158

Routledge is an imprint of the Taylor & Francis Group, an informa business

British Library Cataloguing-in-Publication Data
A catalogue record for this book is available from the British Library

Library of Congress Cataloging-in-Publication Data
Names: Martins, Cristiano Zanin, author. | Martins, Valeska Teixeira Zanin, author. | Valim, Rafael, author. | Boland, Colleen, translator.
Title: Lawfare: waging war through law/Cristiano Zanin Martins, Valeska Teixeira Zanin Martins, Rafael Valim; translated by Colleen Boland; revised by Linda Murur.
Description: Milton Park, Abingdon, Oxon; New York, NY: Routledge, 2021. Includes bibliographical references and index.
Identifiers: LCCN 2021009456 (print) | LCCN 2021009457 (ebook) | ISBN 9780367745141 (hardback) | ISBN 9780367745165 (paperback) | ISBN 9781003158257 (ebook)
Subjects: LCSH: Lawfare. | War. | Government liability. | Government liability (International law) | War (International law) | Public interest law. | Lula, 1945- | Prosecution–Political aspects–Brazil.
Classification: LCC K967 .M38 2021 (print) | LCC K967 (ebook) | DDC 340/.115–dc23
LC record available at https://lccn.loc.gov/2021009456
LC ebook record available at https://lccn.loc.gov/2021009457

ISBN: 978-0-367-74514-1 (hbk)
ISBN: 978-0-367-74516-5 (pbk)
ISBN: 978-1-003-15825-7 (ebk)

Typeset in Times New Roman
by Deanta Global Publishing Services, Chennai, India

Contents

Foreword

Lawfare, as both a concept and a species of political practice, has exploded over the past decades, from the late twentieth century into ours, the twenty-first. Google it, and 1,590,000 results come up in less than half a second.[1] Despite this digital overload, a comprehensive history of the term is yet to be written, although many different points of origin, from the 1950s onwards, are mentioned in the strikingly diffuse literature that has grown up around it.[2] Lawfare proliferates definitions at a giddy rate, some of which cling to the metaphorical, while others lean close to the literal, the empirical, the tactical. Nor is this surprising. These differences reflect a plethora of ideological orientations, right and left alike – and, even more, a wide range of political, juridical, material, moral and particularly military ends.

Of course, unnamed, the phenomenon has a deep past. To take just one example, a British missionary to colonial Southern Africa wrote, in 1887, that local chiefs believed the most fearsome weapons of "the English mode of warfare" to be "'papers' and agents and courts". This, added the evangelist, "was said with contempt".[3] Indeed, alongside the more obviously violent instruments of colonization, the quotidian deployments of the law – of treaty and title, of proclamation and legislation, of contract and covenant, of judicial commissions and the like – introduced indigenous peoples everywhere to the structural violence inherent in the sovereign rule of Empire. In some parts of the colonial world, like West Africa and South Africa, it

---

1 Or at least they did on 27 July 2020. A day later, that number rose to 1,780,000.
2 For some historical background broadly conceived, however, see Craig A. Jones ("Lawfare and the juridification of late modern war". *Progress in Human Geography*, vol. 40, no. 2, pp. 221–239); Orde Kittrie offers a relatively detailed history, but it is tilted almost entirely to the association between lawfare and war, a point to which we return later (*Lawfare*: Law as a weapon of war. New York: Oxford University Press, 2016).
3 MACKENZIE, John. *Austral Africa*: Losing it or ruling it. London: Sampson Low, Marston, Searle & Rivington, 2015, p. 80.

spawned indigenous cadres of lawyers, some of whom used their learned skills *against* ruling regimes (and against their proxies, among them, local chiefs and kings). Today lawfare has a name: a name whose different denotations and connotations, most of them hinting of menace, point to the illegitimate use of coercion under the licit sign of the jural. And much else besides.

The extent to which lawfare has entered into public discourse is staggering. In the USA, for instance, *Lawfare* – a blog put out by the Lawfare Institute of the Brookings Institution – claimed in 2015, in *The New Lawfare*, that it had 490,000 "users", up 90% from the year before; those users, it said, included the Justice Department, the Pentagon, the Senate, the State Department, the CIA and the White House.[4] Three years earlier, *Harvard Law Today* called *Lawfare* "essential reading for leading thinkers on law and security"; indeed, "de rigueur for ... [anyone] influential in the galactic scheme of things".[5] Of late, its content seems all over the place, both geographically and topically. On 21 July 2020,[6] *Lawfare* offered material and commentary on, among other things, digital contact tracing, a US cyberspace report, a decision of the European Court of Justice, US–China technology policy and national security news. It is not easy to establish, from this melange, what is intended to be specifically relevant to lawfare and what refers to the affairs of law at large. But the implicit stress on security does press itself on the roving eye.

Nor is *Lawfare* alone in this new American scholarly marketplace: the brand is widely shared and growing. Already in 2010, *Case Western Reserve Journal of International Law* published a special edition, "Lawfare!" – note the exclamation – itself the yield of a "symposium [of] experts meeting to explore the concept" at Case Western Reserve University School of Law in September that year.[7] Even more than *Lawfare*, the Brookings blog, this initiative was heavily devoted to the relationships among lawfare, war and security. Not surprisingly, it included an essay by Charles J. Dunlap,[8] the

---

4 *The new lawfare*: Hard national security choices, 7 June 2015. Retrieved from: www.brookings.edu/blog/techtank/2015/06/08/welcome-to-the-new-lawfare/. Accessed 18 July 2020. The blog was founded in 2015.

5 BACON, Katie. "All's fair in lawfare", *Harvard Law Today*, 21 December 2012. Retrieved from: https://today.law.harvard.edu/alls-fair-in-lawfare/. Accessed 20 July 2020.

6 www.lawfareblog.com/. Accessed 21 July 2020.

7 The quotation is from the abstract of the foreword to the issue (Scharf and Pagano 2010:1); for the journal issue itself, see *Case Western Reserve Journal of International Law*, vol. 43, no. 1&2, 2010–2011.

8 DUNLAP, Charles. "Does lawfare need an apologia?" *Case Western Reserve Journal of International Law*, vol. 43, no. 1&2, pp. 121–143.

doyen of this scholarly genealogy;[9] that is, the idea of law as a weapon of war, or, more precisely, a weapon of weak enemies "using legal principles dishonestly" to defeat the USA (ironic emphasis). This take on the concept – its negative association with legal efforts to counter the "righteous" conduct of war by the strong against those whom it would defeat – has had its critics. Among them, notably, are David Luban[10] and Scott Horton,[11] who argue that lawfare used in this sense, specifically as propagated by the scholarly and policy progeny of General Dunlap, is a "dangerous game" and a threat to democracy. General Dunlap's point is echoed, implicitly, by the Democracy Fund, which supports another, different Lawfare Institute whose self-appointed mandate is the protection of the US Constitution and its democratic order.[12] Luban and Horton might have added to their critique of lawfare that American administrations have regularly stretched the limits of legality in acting against insurgent enemies, real or imagined; drone killings, waterboarding and other forms of torture, all regarded as repugnant in the civilized world, come to mind – all of them laundered by law to serve the purposes of US military "necessity".

Lawfare, then, in its military–security oriented American sense, speaks as though it were primarily a weapon of the weak against the powerful – and ought to be understood by scholars and statespersons as such – while the powerful, states and global capitals alike, often deploy it to their own ends against whomever they take to be a threat; in the case of the USA, this includes other foreign powers, among them China.[13] A notable non-state example is something that calls itself the Lawfare Project (www.thelawfareproject.org/; www.the lawfare project.org/who-we-are). It is dedicated to "defend[ing] the civil and human rights of the pro-Israeli community"; also, to combatting "'Islamist lawfare' … as a weapon of war" and, more

---

9 See e.g. Charles Dunlap (Law and Military Interventions: Preserving Humanitarian Values in 21st Century Conflicts. Carr Center for Human Rights Policy, Kennedy School of Government, Harvard University (29 November), Washington, DC. Retrieved from: http://people.duke.edu/~pfeaver/dunlap.pdf); also Orde Kittrie (*Lawfare*: Law as a weapon of war. New York: Oxford University Press, 2016).

10 LUBAN, David. "Carl Schmitt and the critique of lawfare". *Case Western Reserve Journal of International Law*, vol. 43, no. 1&2, pp. 457–471.

11 These essays by Horton and Luban are also included in the *Case Western Reserve Journal of International Law* issue on "Lawfare!"

12 "Lawfare Institute", Democracy Fund; https://democracyfund.nclud.com/grant/lawfare-institute/. Accessed 20 July 2020.

13 "Law as a battlefield: The United States, China, and global escalation of lawfare". A Public Seminar at the Belfer Center for Science and International Affairs, Harvard Kennedy School, 6 February 2020. Retrieved from: www.belfercenter.org/event/law-battlefield-united-states-china-and-global-escalation-lawfare. Accessed 11 August 2020.

generally, to fighting against "militant Islam" or anyone anywhere who might act against Jews. Its work, say its New York-based lawyers, "spans the globe". To parody Hobbes, human existence today appears to have become a matter of "the law of all against all". The judicialization of almost everything, even of life itself, makes that parody an uncomfortable reality.

But – and this is where the present volume appears as a critically important intervention on the subject – there are very different ways of understanding lawfare, as Craig Jones[14] points out. Their geopolitical source is, largely at least, the global south, most notably but not limited to South Africa and Brazil. In South Africa, a growing scholarly literature is emerging;[15] it seeks to conceptualize the phenomenon in its various forms, historicize it and analyse its effects on law and society. But more strikingly, the term now appears regularly in the national print and electronic media; it has become a colloquial usage, part of the public sociology of everyday life. What is more, its diffusion into public discourse makes plain the fact that, as an organic phenomenon, it has taken on many modalities, many means and ends, all the more so as a culture of rights and the juridification of politics has come to suffuse civil society – although, as Zanin, Martins and Valim stress in this volume, "lawfare should not be confused with the judicialization of politics", sui generis. It is a more specific, particular species of practice. Its two dominant modalities, however, contrast hegemonic lawfare, perpetrated by powerful states, corporations, non-governmental organizations, religious organizations, ethnic groups and the like, with insurgent lawfare, a Lilliputian form deployed by "little people" against those who oppress, exploit or otherwise violate them, their rights, their property, their being-in-the-world. The latter, self-evidently, is the less common form, and in tournaments of legal force, "little people" are less likely to prevail; there are many places, one scarcely need mention, where they have no access at all to the instruments of the law. Yet this is not always the case, and, where they do have access, they do not always lose – even against more powerful antagonists.[16]

---

14 JONES, Craig A. "Lawfare and the juridification of late modern war". *Progress in Human Geography*, vol. 40, no. 2, pp. 221–239.

15 See e.g. LE ROUX, Michelle and DAVIS, Dennis (*Lawfare*: Judging politics in South Africa. Johannesburg: Jonathan Ball, 2019); CORDER, Hugh and HOEXTER, Cora ("'Lawfare' in South Africa and its effects on the judiciary". *African Journal of Legal Studies*, vol. 10, pp. 105–126).

16 COMAROFF, John; COMAROFF, Jean. "Law and disorder in the postcolony: An introduction". *In: Law and disorder in the postcolony*. Chicago: University of Chicago Press, 2006, pp. 26–31.

It is deep into hegemonic form that *Lawfare: Waging War through Law* takes us. Its authors, Cristiano Zanin, Valeska Martins and Rafael Valim – at whose initiative a global southern Lawfare Institute (www.lawfareinstitute.com) was founded in São Paulo and launched in London in 2017 – offer an unsparing, important treatment of the phenomenon. Their scholarship has a strong activist component, in major measure motivated by a commitment to the rule of both law and justice. It has also been honed by their legal struggle on behalf of former President Lula against the violent legal excesses of a right-wing Brazilian regime that did everything it could to sentence him to political and social death. Part conceptual and analytic, part empirical – it discusses cases in the global north as well – the book treats lawfare not as a metaphor, but as an exceptionally complex species of political practice whose brute analogy to war explains a great deal; like war, "its purpose is the delegitimizing, harming, or annihilating an enemy" – and not only in military contexts, but in a late modern world of the "law of all against all". Those nineteenth-century African chiefs who understood law as "the English mode of warfare" were prescient. For them, too, lawfare was not a metaphor. It was, indeed, an instrument of annihilation. A hundred and forty years later, that "mode of warfare" is becoming planetary. *Lawfare: Waging War through Law* is an essential guide to its inner workings, its rationalities, its effects.

John Comaroff
Harvard University

Preface

This book was conceived, indisputably, out of what has been considered the most emblematic case of lawfare today: the criminal persecution of former President Luiz Inácio Lula da Silva.[1] There are positive and negative aspects regarding this. On the one hand, we have had access to an extraordinary universe of empirical data that both inspired and confirmed a series of theoretical hypotheses. On the other hand, because of the repercussions of the case and its political, commercial and geopolitical disputes, the theoretical debate can be marred with distortions and rhetoric.

Lawfare is not just a slogan, a method or a game at the service of any one political ideology. Really, it has to do with a complex, multifaceted phenomenon that should be carefully reflected upon in modern constitutional democracies, given that it is able to demolish, in one fell swoop, majority rule and the rule of law.

There is also the argument that lawfare is restricted to the political domain and it is confused with judicial activism. As we will see over the course of this book, lawfare can victimize anyone subject to the law, including corporation executives.

The literature specializing in the subject, as a general rule, alternates between analysis of only one aspect of the phenomenon or consists of extensive case studies. It is for this reason that we have made a great effort to offer, although in an initial form, a theoretical text that approaches the theme broadly; applying a multifaceted way in which to present lawfare in its actuality.

1 HOUNET, Yazid ben. "Lawfare: pourquoi il faut prendre Jean-Luc Mélenchon au sérieux". Retrieved from: www.liberation.fr/debats/2019/09/24/lawfare-pourquoi-il-faut-prendre-jean-luc-melenchon-au-serieux_1753110. Accessed 4 September 2019.

Naturally, we were not just inspired by mere interest. It is in this decisive historic moment in which, undeniably, coups and consequences are being meted on our civilizations, that we should reveal lawfare, as well as the ways to confront it, in a way that re-establishes the real significance of the law. This is exactly what the reader will find in the pages of this book.

Cristiano Zanin
Valeska Martins
Rafael Valim

Introduction

We have witnessed many indications, beginning in 2013, that something wrong has been instilled in our country. During that year, protests took place that were apparently organized on social media by indifferent individuals who would not normally engage in activism.[1] The public also learned over the course of that year that documents from the United States National Security Agency (NSA) indicated that the USA had spied on Petrobras, dozens of Brazilian authorities in the highest echelons of the Republic and on the President of the Republic, Dilma Rousseff, herself.

The country's political and social environment worsened during this period. In 2014, it experienced a presidential election that profoundly polarized the country. As soon as the former President of the Republic, Dilma Rousseff, was re-elected, this was quickly called into question by the losing candidate Aécio Neves, heightening political and social tensions. The process of impeaching Dilma Rousseff began in December 2015, which would lead to her definitive departure in August 2016.

During the period in which the impeachment of Dilma Rousseff took place, we took on and led the technical defence of former President Luiz Inácio Lula da Silva. We confronted the various frivolous and unsubstantiated investigations he faced, especially by the Federal Police and the Federal Public Ministry of the Federal District (Brasilia) and of Curitiba. We confirmed that the actions carried out by those authorities under the pretext that the investigation would lead to hypothesized accusations were conducted in tandem with a vocal contingent of the mainstream media and alongside a turbulent political period in our country. This situation went a long way to amplify the evil effects of these investigations that, strictly speaking, could not even be substantiated, given the complete absence of

---

1 It is very possible that these protests were initiated or influenced via the use and manipulation of personal data.

real and objective evidence that could point towards any criminal activity committed by the former president. We assert that in this way, we are facing something different. It was not a simple case in which we had to defend a client who was being investigated by the state's prosecutor bodies for alleged commitment of crimes. We were facing persecution instigated by agents of the justice system, including police, members of the public ministries and judges, aligned with some of the most influential media, with the objective of manipulating the political situation. These acts were orchestrated with the clear objective of destabilizing and destroying an elected government, as well as with the intention of preventing the politically popular, former President of the Republic, Luiz Inácio Lula da Silva, from remaining in the electoral race. The objective of annihilation was clear, both from a personal and political point of view.

These circumstances have led us to conduct an extensive study, not only into the cases in which investigations were substantiated, but also via a survey of literature available on the use or abuse of the law to achieve political or illegitimate ends.

In Brazil, work regarding the abuse of the law or the abuse of authority and other related subjects did not comprehensively outline all the characteristics of the situation that we are facing. At the international level, when researching in the United States at the beginning of 2016, we found the work *Lawfare: Law as a weapon of war*, written by Orde F. Kittrie.

Kittrie's work sought to demonstrate that laws and legal procedures were used by non-state entities and even groups outside of the realm of the law to achieve effects similar to military action against the US State. In other words, the law was used as a weapon, for kinetic warfare both in the United States and in territories where Americans were involved in a conflict. The book echoed the understanding of the great American general Charles J. Dunlap Jr, who coined the term "lawfare".

Thus, the book's approach meant critically analyzing what is taking place in Brazil – the laws and legal procedures manipulated to serve as a weapon of war against former President Lula and his political allies. Public opinion and society have been influenced so as to make the attack on Lula viable – with the aim of preventing his participation in politics and allowing a new form of power to install itself in our country.

Our investigation found validation from renowned American professors. Jean and John Comaroff[2] affirmed our vision and shared their empirical and academic experiences living in South Africa during apartheid and

2 Professors of African Studies, African American Studies and Anthropology at Harvard University.

the imprisonment of Nelson Mandela, which they expanded upon once in the United States. We engaged in an intense exchange of experiences with them. Moreover, we were in contact at that time with David W. Kennedy, a distinguished Harvard University Professor of International Law. He was of great assistance in our rereading of lawfare from the point of view of Brazil, as well as of similar manifestations of it throughout Latin America.

During this reflective period, in studying at the university libraries and in interviewing the eminent professor, we found that no one had addressed lawfare in Brazil, which made our research and work even more challenging.

On 10 October 2016, during a press conference we held at our law firm to discuss former President Lula's case, we introduced the concept of law-fare to the various journalists present, both from domestic and international outlets. At the time, we defined it as the perverse utilization of the law and legal procedures to prosecute enemies and opponents for illegitimate ends. In Lula's case, the objectives were both political and geopolitical, related to the discovery and exploitation of the pre-salt oil region as was later confirmed.

Our studies continued and other press interviews and journal publications regarding the subject followed. We engaged in intense academic debates with the co-author of this book and friend, about lawfare and its scientific aspects. Together with Rafael Valim, a scholar and connoisseur of public law and in particular the state of exception, we organized the knowledge regarding this question, expanding our theoretical repertoire, and arrived at conclusions presented in this work.

We also posit, based on the in-depth analysis of the subject, that lawfare utilizes unconventional forms of warfare, in everything from military, to geopolitical, political and commercial disputes, in order to obtain illegiti-mate ends.[3] Lawfare is one of the ways that "hybrid wars" manifest them-selves, noted in the US army manual since 2018 (TC 18-01).

In addition to our work in what, in our view, represents the most exten-sive case of lawfare in progress, that of former President Lula, we have researched and analyzed other cases with the same characteristics, with geopolitical, political or economic purposes. We also established dur-ing this governmental impasse, together with Rafael Valim, the Lawfare

---

3 The journalist Fausto Macedo, in the publication *O Estado de S. Paulo*, for example, sum-marized the interview as such: "The former President's lawyers affirm that the district attorneys who charged him with corruption and money-laundering in the triplex case using 'lawfare tactics'". Retrieved from: https://politica.estadao.com.br/blogs/fausto-macedo/def esa-de-lula-diz-que-lava-jato-usa-leis-como-arma-de-guerra-para-desmoralizar-inimigo/. Accessed 3 September 2019.

Institute;[4] an entity that convenes both Brazilian and international scholars in the fields of law, sociology, anthropology, communications and psychology, to study concrete cases of lawfare in order to develop and disseminate academic literature regarding this phenomenon. The Lawfare Institute has already produced reports examining specific international cases, including that of former Ecuadorian President Rafael Correa. The Institute also holds collaborative agreements with several universities, providing courses on the subject and facilitating the expansion of this field of study, as well as its debate.

The study and development of concrete cases involving the Foreign Corrupt Practices Act (FCPA), a United States law used to extend its own power in order to punish and collect securities outside its jurisdictions, provided examples of another medium in which the practice of lawfare was frequently used.

Therefore, this book proposes to introduce lawfare into the national and international debate based on a review we made of intensive studies on the subject. It is also rooted in our experience not only in defending former President Lula, but also in other specific cases either as lawyers or in our capacity as founders of the Lawfare Institute.

Finally, before the reader proceeds to delve deeper into the subject, we would caution: lawfare should not be confused with the judicialization of politics, nor is it something that only pertains to the Brazilian or Latin American left. On the contrary, lawfare is coupled with new forms of war and disputes instigated mainly in the United States, and any person, institution or government can be a victim. Whether geopolitical, political or economic conflict, it involves individuals from the justice system, as well as other organs that relate to the law, willing to manipulate laws and legal procedures to achieve illegitimate ends using various resources for persuasion.

In short, we emphasize that the objective of this book is not to provide an exhaustive account of the subject, but rather to formally initiate a discussion of this highly relevant phenomenon, which a diverse range of professionals from leaders to executives to businesspeople can address.

Cristiano Zanin
Valeska Martins

---

4 See the website of the Lawfare Institute: www.lawfareinstitute.com.

1   What is lawfare?

The most elementary questions are, by principle, the ones that are the most challenging. Regarding the topic we are now discussing, many assert that a given situation is a case of lawfare, but they cannot answer the following question: what is lawfare?

Given this objectionable position, in this first chapter we will outline our definition of lawfare.

1.1 The origins and evolution of the concept

The neologism "lawfare" is a compound of the words law and warfare. One of the first records of it can be traced back to an article published by John Carlson and Neville Yeomans in 1975,[1] in which it is posited that "lawfare substitutes war, and harm is made with words, not swords".

Lawfare also finds its origins in the work *Unrestricted warfare*, written by two officials from the People's Liberation Army of China, in which lawfare takes on a secondary role alongside other alternate forms of war including psychological, information, technological and economic. For the authors war encompasses a broad range in modernity, with politics as only one of its manifestations.[2]

The work, however, popularized the term "lawfare" and guided its discussion. In recent years, US Air Force Colonel Charles Dunlap argued in 2001 that "'lawfare' that is, the use of law as a weapon of war, is the newest

---

1 CARLSON, John; YEOMANS, Neville. "Whither goeth the law: Humanity or barbarity". *In*: SMITH, Margareth; CROSSLEY, David (Eds). *The way out*: Radical alternatives in Australia. Melbourne: Lansdowne Press, 1975. Retrieved from: www.laceweb.org.au/whi .htm. Accessed 3 September 2019.
2 LIANG, Qiao; XIANGSUI, Wang. *Unrestricted warfare*. Beijing: PLA Literature and Arts Publishing House, 1999, pp. 190 and 191.

feature of 21st century combat".[3] In this article, the author uses the label of "lawfare" to critique the strategic use of the law, in particular International Human Rights Law, to delegitimize military campaigns in the United States and Israel, which represented a threat to national security in those countries.[4] In effect, it is no coincidence that the National Defense Strategy published by the Pentagon in March 2005 said that the law "is a weapon of the weak used in judicial processes and terrorism to undermine America".[5] Another member of the US government at the time argued that the "real" abuse of the law in Guantánamo was not conducted by those who undertook and authorized the torture, but rather by "illegal enemy combatants".

Subsequently, Dunlap himself attempted to define lawfare neutrally,[6] with the idea that not only could the enemy use it, but it could also benefit national security in the United States. This would be because it is "preferable to the bloody, expensive and destructive forms of war that devastated the world in the 20th century". The law could be a weapon or, in this sense, could be used to achieve good or bad purposes.

So, lawfare became a "strategy of using – or misusing – law as a substitute for traditional military means to achieve an operational object".[7]

In the same year (2001) when Charles Dunlap's important article came to light, American anthropologist John Comaroff proposed another concept for the term lawfare. For him, it meant, "the use of force to conquer and control indigenous populations through coercive use of legal means".[8] In this way, Comaroff transfers the weapon from the hands of the colonized into the hands of the colonizer. In 2007, John Comaroff and Jean Comaroff revisited the matter and described lawfare as "recourse to legal instruments, with the violence inherent in the Law, to commit acts of political coercion".[9] They also interpreted lawfare as a "Lilliputian strategy" – that is, lawfare as

---

3 DUNLAP JR., Charles J. "Law and military interventions: Preserving humanitarian values in 21st century conflicts". Working Paper, Cambridge (Mass.), Harvard University, John F. Kennedy School of Government, 2001, p. 2.

4 WERNER, Wouter G. "The curious career of lawfare". *Case Western Reserve Journal of International Law*, no. 43, 2010, p. 62.

5 The National Defense Strategy of The United States of America. Retrieved from: https:// archive. defense.gov/news/Mar2005/ d20050318nds1.pdf. Accessed 3 September 2019.

6 KITTRIE, Orde F. *Lawfare: Law as a weapon of war*. Oxford: Oxford University Press, 2016, p. 6.

7 DUNLAP JR, Charles J. "Lawfare today: A perspective". *Yale Journal of International Affairs*, 2008, p. 146.

8 COMAROFF, John L. "Colonialism, culture, and the law: A foreword". *Law & Social Inquiry*, vol. 26, p. 306.

9 COMAROFF, Jean; COMAROFF, John. "Law and disorder in postcolony". *Social Anthropology/Anthropologie Sociale*, vol. 15, p. 144.

an insurgency strategy used by vulnerable groups. This would be a neoliberal capture of politics, endangering claims to the very rights in question.[10]

In 2016, Orde Kittrie published the work *Lawfare: Law as a weapon of war* and, based on the teaching of Charles Dunlap, sought the perfect definition of lawfare, classifying it into two elements: (1) using the law to obtain effects similar to those obtained via conventional military action; (2) the action must be motivated by a desire to weaken or destroy the adversary.[11]

Finally, in 2017, Siri Gloppen presented a strict concept of lawfare and defined it as "mobilization of legal strategies that include some form of litigation, with the motive of social transformation beyond victory via an individual judicial process".[12] The form of insurgent lawfare described by Jean and John Comaroff resonates with this definition, but without the critical connotation they apply. Lawfare is characterized as the legitimate use of strategic litigation to achieve political and social objectives.

Currently, it only takes a simple investigation to discover innumerable writings on lawfare, especially in English, outlining one of the concepts we have just provided. However, as 2016 came to a close, we began to build a new definition of lawfare, which, as we will see later, although it has some similarities with the other definitions, should not be confused with them.

1.2 The Lula case: a new definition emerges

The criminal prosecution of former President Luiz Inácio Lula da Silva caused a profound paradigm shift, not only in Brazilian law, but also, and especially, in the Brazilian justice system.

Before, there were no procedural errors or errors of adjudication in the judiciary. There was a clear method and purpose to all the state's procedural acts, and action taken outside of formal processes to instrumentalize the law so as to destroy what was considered the enemy, in an unprecedented manner.

This unprecedented phenomenon needed a name, and lawfare was undoubtedly the most eloquent designation for the true legal war that had

10 COMAROFF, Jean; COMAROFF, John L. *Ethnicity, Inc.* Chicago: University of Chicago Press, 2009, p. 55.
11 KITTRIE, Orde F. *Lawfare:* Law as a weapon of war. Oxford: Oxford University Press, 2016, p. 8.
12 GLOPPEN, Siri. *Conceptualizing lawfare*, p. 14. Retrieved from: www.academia.edu/356 08212/Conceptualizing_ Lawfare_A_Typology_and_Theoretical_Framwork. Accessed 3 September 2019.

been declared. From that moment on, lawfare meant *the strategic use of law with the purpose of delegitimizing, harming or annihilating an enemy.*[13]

In that sense, the term was quickly disseminated throughout Latin America and incorporated into legal and political lexicons, in the context of a proliferation of great operations mounted to "combat" corruption. At the same time, there was a birth of an incipient legal literature on the subject, notable for its confusion between lawfare and the phenomenon of judicializing politics.

On 4 June 2019, Pope Francis, in his speech to the Pan-American Judges' Summit on Social Rights and Franciscan Doctrine, explicitly employed the vocabulary of "lawfare" and pointed to our own semantics:[14]

> to express to you my concern about a new form of exogenous intervention in the political scenarios of countries through the misuse of legal procedures and judicial classification. In addition to putting countries' democracies in serious danger, lawfare is generally used to undermine emerging political processes and to tend toward the systematic violation of Social Rights. In order to guarantee the institutional quality of States, it is fundamental to detect and neutralize these types of practices which stem from improper judicial activity in combination with parallel multimedia operations.

More recently, on 7 September 2019, Jean-Luc Mélenchon, leader of La France Insoumise party, along with over 150 signatories led a manifesto that denounced lawfare using the Lula case as one of the main examples of this as a global phenomenon, saying, "Examples are numerous. In South America, the Brazilian Lula was sentenced without evidence and prevented from standing in the presidential election. The acting judge, Sergio Moro, has since become Minister of Justice for far-right President Jair Bolsonaro".[15]

However, the *use* of the concept is always problematic, as it is inevitably influenced by the context in which it takes place, and given the examples above, we apply a *critical view* when considering lawfare.

---

13 Section 1.4 of this chapter deals with this definition.
14 FRANCISCO. *Discurso del Santo Padre Francisco en la Cumbre de Jueces Panamericanos sobre derechos sociales y doctrina franciscana.* Retrieved from: http://w2.vatican.va/cont ent/francesco/es/speeches/2019/june/documents/papa-francesco_20190604_giudici-pa namericani.html?fbclid=IwAR1u0b1OogQqzfCylPYbSr13S-_mz_clj4JtcDjMEbsDO TpFzs_3jFLkcDY. Accessed 3 September 2019.
15 *Stop lawfare.* Retrieved from: https://lawfare.fr/. Accessed 7 September 2019.

1.3 Theoretical framework: a strategic perspective

It is acknowledged that the law, in its complexity, does not give forth a single knowledge, but provides various specific knowledge with regards to the cognitive subject. The law can be divided into several objects of study, each with its own methodology, which draw their validity from the consistency on which the knowledge is built.[16]

One potential aspect of the law which has only recently been explored, is *strategy*. In other words, the law becomes the object of the science of strategy.[17]

The dogmatic, sociological, philosophical and economic views of the law are well known, but what would a strategic reading of the law consist of? To answer that question we must focus, albeit briefly, on the notion of *strategy*.

The word itself derives from the Greek word *estrategos*, which means general, commander or leader of the troops.[18] In the work of André Beaufre, strategy is described in one of its most cited definitions as: "the art of the dialectic of two opposing wills using force to resolve their dispute".[19]

Although the contemporary theoretical concept of strategy extends to a variety of domains,[20] its original and authentic object is war, which in Clausewitz's classical understanding, translates to "an act of violence intended to force the adversary into submitting to our will".[21]

Strictly speaking, when we reflect on the term "strategy", we are alluding to the imposition of one will on another by force. Again, as André Beaufre teaches us, "in this dialectic of wills, it is a psychological effect produced in

---

16 VALIM, Rafael. *O princípio da segurança jurídica no Direito Administrativo brasileiro.* São Paulo: Malheiros, 2010, p. 23.

17 For the debate in regard to the status of strategy, see: FERNANDES, António Horta. *O Homo estrategicus ou a ilusão de uma razão estratégica?* Lisbon: Edições Cosmos, 1998, p. 182.

18 SAINT-PIERRE, Hector Luis. "Estratégia". *In:* SAINT-PIERRE, Héctor Luis; VITELLI, Marina Gisela (Eds). *Dicionário de segurança e defesa.* São Paulo: Editora Unesp, Imprensa Oficial do Estado de São Paulo, 2018, p. 369.

19 BEAUFRE, André. *Introduction a la stratégie.* Paris: Librairie Armand Colin, 1963, p. 16.

20 António Horta Fernandes observes: "Use of the term 'strategy' has been banalized today. From business strategy, to football strategy, the term extends indefinitely, not only due to the ease of its ordinary use, but also in institutional forums, where it is utilized in serious documents, intending to convey everything but at the same time conveying nothing" (FERNANDES, António Horta. *O Homo estrategicus ou a ilusão de uma razão estratégica?* Lisbon: Edições Cosmos, 1998, p. 129). In the same sense: MARTINS, Raúl François. *Acerca do conceito de estratégia.* Lisbon: IDN, 1984, p. 99; DESPORTES, Vincent. "La stratégie en theories". *Politique étrangère,* 2014/2, p. 165.

21 CLAUSEWITZ, Carl von. *Da guerra.* 3rd ed. São Paulo: Martins Fontes, 2014, p. 7.

the enemy: when he becomes convinced that it is useless to start or alternatively to continue in the fight".[22]

In this way, strategy involves classifying and prioritizing events with the intent of choosing the most effective means to obtain certain objectives. It is a "discipline of means" serving political and economic interests. A fundamental component of strategy and one that we are particularly interested in is *hostility*. Strategic thinking is not characterized by a mere contrast of will or interests.[23] It is much more than this; he who manifests an opposing will is treated with hostility, like an enemy to be defeated through threats or coercive measures.[24] As Clausewitz says, the immediate objective of war is to "*throw* his opponent in order to make him incapable of further resistance".[25]

It is also essential to establish a classic distinction between *strategy* and *tactics*, which has important consequences for lawfare.

1.3.1 The distinction between strategy and tactics

There is a common assertion that tactics direct the action of *combat*, while strategy amalgamates such combat to achieve the ends of *war*.[26] In more abstract terms, in 1892 General Bonnal offered the following differentiation between strategy and tactics: "strategy is the art of conceiving; tactics is the science of execution".[27]

In this way, tactics is more detailed and contingent; inherently limited in time and space and aimed at solving a specific problem.[28] Strategy, on the other hand, includes the entire campaign within which the choice of tactics, to an extent, takes on a certain degree of rigidity.

So, although tactics are subordinate to strategy, there is a clear *reciprocity* between the concepts. Strategy determines tactics, which in turn affects strategy. As António Horta Fernandes astutely observes, "strategy commands the measures taken in tactics, guides them, and does not presuppose them as a mere aggregate of tactical actions, but instead tactics also affect

22 BEAUFRE, André. *Introduction a la stratégie*. Paris: Librairie Armand Colin, 1963, p. 16.
23 DESPORTES, Vincent. "La stratégie en theories". *Politique étrangère*, 2014, p. 168.
24 MARTINS, Raúl François: "la estrategia es el arte de controlar y utilizar los recursos de un país – o de una coalición – incluso sus fuerzas armadas, a fin de promover y asegurar efectivamente sus intereses vitales contra los enemigos, actuales, potenciales o apenas supuestos" (*Acerca do conceito de estratégia*. Lisbon: IDN, 1984, p. 109).
25 CLAUSEWITZ, Carl von. *Da guerra*, 3rd ed. São Paulo: Martins Fontes, 2014, p. 7.
26 DESPORTES, Vincent. "La stratégie en theories". *Politique étrangère*, 2014, p. 168.
27 MARTINS, Raúl François. *Acerca do conceito de estratégia*. Lisbon: IDN, 1984, p. 104.
28 DESPORTES, Vincent. "La stratégie en theories". *Politique étrangère*, 2014, p. 170.

strategy, with radical modifications from one tactical phenomenon to the next, which must logically lead to different strategies". [29]

We can conclude then, that politics or economics subordinate strategy, and this in turn subordinates tactics.[30] This concept is key in understanding lawfare.

1.4 Definition

As is generally recognized, definitions and classifications are not *true* or *false* but rather are either *useful* or *not useful*. Therefore, they are meeting a criterion of *utility*, that is to say their value lies in presenting a reality in an understandable way.[31]

Naturally, the concept of lawfare must also be viewed through the epistemological lens. A single event or mere desire[32] does not justify a new definition or classification.

Lawfare is a deliberate concept illuminating and transforming a concrete reality that, despite its great importance, was up until now obscured. In other words, no other concept adequately explains the phenomenon that lawfare refers to, and this is the reason we must procure it.

But ultimately, how do we define lawfare? In its strictest sense, lawfare is the strategic use of the law with the purpose of delegitimizing, harming or annihilating the enemy.

An analysis of this definition follows in order to understand its various elements.

The first of these is the *strategic use of the law*. In effect, if we consider the original and authentic meaning of strategy that we have already outlined, lawfare could be defined as simply this element. This is because when we say it is the strategic use of the law, it is immediately inferred that legal norms become weapons intended for certain enemies.

---

29 FERNANDES, António Horta. *O* Homo estrategicus *ou a ilusão de uma razão estratégica?* Lisbon: Edições Cosmos, 1998, p. 220.

30 As Luigi Bonanate asserts: "In this sense, just as strategy is subordinated to politics, similarly tactics is and cannot avoid being subordinate to strategy. Tactic is precisely the means of applying strategy. The task of strategic leadership is, in effect, a prudent selection of means (tactics), which always involves the use or threat of using physical force, to achieve the objectives indicated by the politics" (BONANATE, Luigi. "Strategy and politics, two weapons". *In*: BOBBIO, Norberto; MATTEUCCI, Nicola; PASQUINO, Gianfranco (Eds). *Dictionary of politics*, vol. 1, 13th ed. Brazil: Editorial University of Brazil, 2010, p. 432).

31 CARRIÓ, Genaro. *Notes on law and language.* 3rd ed. Buenos Aires: Abeledo-Perrot, 1986, p. 99.

32 WERNER, Wouter G. "The curious career of lawfare". *Case Western Reserve Journal of International Law*, vol. 43, 2010, p. 63.

However, the banalization of the concept of strategy means we must expand upon the definition, even with the risk of it being redundant. We cannot fail to signal the meaning of the strategic use of law. It is public knowledge that force and the law go together. As Hans Kelsen puts it,

Force and the Law are not mutually exclusive. Law is the organization of force".[33] However, this is not about the relationship between force and the law. The mandate of law is to regulate and limit the use of force, constituting a technique for the peaceful resolution of disputes. As Luigi Ferrajoli explains, *"law is an instrument in the service of peace.*[34]

Therefore, managing the violence of the law as a means to impose one's will on a certain enemy is incongruent with law and rights themselves;[35] in other words, *using the law as an instrument of war is a radical contradiction.*[36] We can therefore affirm that lawfare translates to a complete voiding of the law.[37] In this way, it is not a *neutral* phenomenon, which could be used either for praiseworthy or reprehensible purposes.[38] Lawfare, in our understanding, *always has a negative connotation* as a phenomenon that denies the law.

We would like to emphasize that the use of "law" in the definition is meant to indicate all legal norms. Legislative acts – either jurisdictional or

---

33 KELSEN, Hans. *A paz pelo direito.* São Paulo: WMF Martins Fontes, 2011.
34 FERRAJOLI, Luigi. *Razones jurídicas del pacifismo.* Madrid: Editorial Trotta, 2004, pp. 28–29.
35 CLAUSEWITZ, Carl von. *Da guerra.* 3rd ed. São Paulo: Martins Fontes, 2014, p. 8.
36 FERRAJOLI, Luigi. *Razones jurídicas del pacifismo.* Madrid: Editorial Trotta, 2004, p. 45.
37 It is interesting to examine David Kennedy's reflection, which posits that in the context of war, the law always loses its legitimacy (KENNEDY, David. *Of war and law.* Princeton: Princeton University Press, 2006, p. 136).
38 Dennis Davis and Michelle Le Roux argue for a neutral sense of lawfare: "Lawfare should be understood as having a duality to it; it can be a good or a bad thing. It is a good thing for adjudication to be political, in the sense that it advances the constitutional project and is undertaken by litigants and judges as an instrument to ensure that the constitutional vision" (LE ROUX, Michelle; DAVIS, Dennis. *Lawfare*: Judging politics in South Africa. Johannesburg: Jonathan Ball Publishers, 2019). Similarly, Charles Dunlap understood: "All of this indicates that – on balance – lawfare in its many forms has been much more of a positive force than a negative one. It has illuminated the role of law in armed conflict in new ways and to new audiences. True, like a weapon it will from time to time be employed wrongly and abusively, but that need not become the norm. Lawfare's utility is optimized when it is used consistently with its original purpose of communicating to non-specialists how law might be used as a positive good in modern war as a substitute for traditional arms" (DUNLAP JR, Charles J. "Does lawfare need an apologia?" *Case Western Reserve Journal of International Law*, vol. 43, no. 2, 2010, p. 142).

administrative, as well as their application by legislative, jurisdictional or administrative bodies, can wipe out the phenomenon of lawfare.

We also provide a definition of lawfare, although we do so in a deliberately redundant manner to indicate the objectives of this strategic use of the law. That is to say, to harm, delegitimize or destroy the enemy.

Now, in a true constitutional democracy in any form, the enemy does not actually exist.[39] Everyone is entitled to rights and equal treatment from public authorities. Lawfare, however, as Zaffaroni demonstratively expresses in addressing the aspect of the enemy, "smuggles the dynamics of war into the rule of law",[40] separating, as indicated in the renowned binomial of Carl Schmitt, *friends* who recognize fundamental rights from *enemies*, who deprive the human condition of such rights.[41]

However, when we analyze lawfare in legal terms, we see it becomes worse than a war between nation states. This is what Public International Law addresses, recognizing a series of rights and duties of the warring parties. With lawfare under the guise of the judiciary, all types of atrocities are committed without limit.

Once the definition of lawfare is revealed, it becomes clear that it is not a *legal concept*. In the work of Professor Celso Antônio Bandeira de Mello, it is used as a relational term regarding norms; a unified point of the law's effects.[42] That is to say, categorizing any given case as lawfare does not *automatically* entail legal effects like, for example, the nullification of judicial or administrative proceedings.

In effect, it is a concept that comes from *a point of view external to the law*,[43] through which the legal experience is analyzed in broader terms with the assistance of various specific knowledge. The concept of lawfare, at once *encourages the "strategization" of the law, and reveals via the science of strategy, the workings of how legal norms are instrumentalized for purposes of war.*

An internal view of the law – dogmatic and legal – would be unable to expose the manipulation of the law conducted by lawfare, especially as the

---

39 Zaffaroni affirms: "the legal concept of enemy is only allowed in an authoritarian state" (ZAFFARONI, E. Raúl. *O inimigo no Direito Penal*. 2nd ed. Rio de Janeiro: Revan, 2007, p. 160).

40 ZAFFARONI, E. Raúl. *O inimigo no Direito Pena*. 2nd ed. Rio de Janeiro: Revan, 2007, p. 25.

41 SCHMITT, Carl. *La notion de politique*. Paris: Flammarion, 1992, p. 64.

42 BANDEIRA DE MELLO, Celso Antônio. *Curso de Direito Administrativo*. 34th ed. São Paulo: Malheiros, 2019, p. 384.

43 HART, Herbert L. A. *O conceito de Direito*. 5th ed. Lisbon: Fundação Calouste Gulbenkian, 2007, p. 99.

validity or invalidity of legal acts do not matter in legal battles. *What is truly of relevance are the tactical or strategic results, which to obtain them, legal or illegal means are adopted indiscriminately.*

1.5 The contiguous categories

When outlining the semantics of the term lawfare, it is now necessary to explain the contiguous categories that, although they have traits in common with the phenomenon, are not to be confused with the concept.

The banalization of the term lawfare in legal and political universes adds to the importance of rigorously conceptualizing it and consequently distinguishing it from adjacent concepts.

1.5.1 The state of exception

The first category frequently articulated alongside the concept of lawfare is that of the *state of exception*.

We are not going to go further into a full examination of the state of exception as it would go beyond the scope of the current study; rather, we will only overview those points related to lawfare.

From the varied approaches to analyzing the issue of the state of exception, a common concept emerges. It is encapsulated in the idea that *some state configurations, due to some sort of abnormality, impact a situation outside of the normative solution that has been designated for it.*[44] In other words: some situations are dealt with according to the will of the jurisdiction or authority deciding the specific case, in a manner that works outside of the limits established by the rule of law.

In light of Carl Schmitt's famous quote – "the sovereign is he who decides on the exception"[45] – we can delineate the three central elements of the state of exception: *sovereignty, superseding norms* and the *enemy*. The sovereign conforms the legal order to his will and as such can except himself from it to neutralize his enemies.

The state of exception and lawfare have precisely in common the figure of the enemy. Both presuppose hostility, the possibility of fighting a virtual enemy, constantly redefining, and withdrawing in some cases, its status as a

---

44 VALIM, Rafael. *Estado de exceção*: a forma jurídica do neoliberalismo. São Paulo: Editora Contracorrente, 2017, p. 25.
45 SCHMITT, Carl. *Political theology*: Four chapters on the concept of sovereignty. Chicago: University of Chicago Press, 2005, p. 5.

person and reducing it to something generic, total and unreal. In Hobbes we find an enlightening passage regarding the *enemy*:[46]

> Lastly, harm inflicted upon one that is a declared enemy falls not under the name of punishment: because seeing they were either never subject to the law, and therefore cannot transgress it; or having been subject to it, and professing to be no longer so, by consequence deny they can transgress it, all the harms that can be done them must be taken as acts of hostility. But in declared hostility all infliction of evil is lawful.

Despite this commonality, it would be incorrect to equate lawfare with the state of exception. Strictly speaking, as we will see in the following, *the state of exception is one of the tactics employed in the second dimension of lawfare*. Comparable with armament, if there is no legal norm facilitating war, an *ad hoc* one is created using the technique of exception.

1.5.2 Judicial activism

Another category dialoguing with lawfare includes *judicial activism* which many term – in our opinion, mistakenly – the judicialization of politics.

It is worthwhile to note the observation of Lenio Luiz Streck with respect to the distinction between judicial activism and the judicialization of politics:[47]

> And so, it is necessary to differentiate between judicial activism and judicialization of politics, an issue that Brazil has addressed in little depth, as if these phenomena dealt with the same thing. The conceptual difficulty should be addressed, especially as we live in a democratic regime, for which the consequences of activism could be very harmful. In that sense, it is possible to affirm that judicialization of politics is a phenomenon, at the same time inexorable and contingent, as it draws from socio-political conditions, as well as from the intervention of the Judicial Power given insufficient intervention from the other Powers. On the other hand, activism takes place within the legal system itself, and consists of an act of will by the one who judges, that is to say, when a "corruption" is defined among the relationship between the Powers,

---

46 HOBBES, Thomas. *Leviatã*. 3rd ed. São Paulo: Martins Fontes, 2014, p. 265.
47 STRECK, Lenio Luiz. *Verdade e consenso*: Constituição, hermenêutica e teorias discursivas. 6th ed. São Paulo: Saraiva, 2017. Kindle Edition.

effected beyond of the jurisdiction of the Judiciary, by way of a decision based on non-legal criteria.

Judicial activism lies in disregarding normative texts and instead relying on personal conviction to interpret. This assumes various labels: "sense of justice", "voice of the people", "the common good", "the public interest", among others, which of course represent a complete subverting of a constitutional democracy. There is no good or bad activism. Hijacking legal texts with interpretations no matter the good intentions of the actor, will always be harmful for the rule of law and democracy.

Judicialization of politics is a sociological fact; a derivation of the character of modern constitutions whose norms advance political, economic and social order. The real problem lies in the *response* of the justice system to the judicialization of politics. If the response draws from ideological preferences and/or personal interpretations, we have judicial activism.

Lawfare, particularly lawfare of a political nature, is permeated by judicial activism that seeks to "fight corruption". This is one of its preferred realms, from which it derives profound distortions of the democratic dynamic via the fraudulent sanctification or demonization of political actors.[48]

As such, the concept of legal activism is far from exposing the phenomenon of lawfare. The *strategization* of law conducted by lawfare is in keeping with the doctrine of judicial activism and in this way, the two concepts should not be confused.

1.5.3 Hybrid wars

War conducted via various dimensions is no novelty. But the concept of hybrid warfare surfaces more clearly in the context of the waves of protest that began in 2010, throughout various countries in the Arab world and then reaching Europe and Latin America.

At first, these protests were supported by the international community, with various specialists and think tank experts doing so under generic labels like "democracy", "freedom" and "fighting corruption".

Upon closer examination, however, we can verify that these were not spontaneous events but were generated by a model of war that is characterized by a combination of military, communications, legal and psychological components that replace traditional means of battle.

---

48 MARAVALL, José María. "Rule of Law as a political weapon". *In*: MARAVALL, José María; PRZEWORSKI, Adam (Eds). *Democracy and the Rule of Law*. Cambridge: Cambridge University Press, 2003, p. 262.

The United States clearly saw that hybrid war, rather than conventional war, was conducted indirectly. For example, in a 2014 speech of former United States President Barack Obama, he affirmed, "The American Military cannot be the only component of our leadership. The fact that we have the best hammer does not mean that every problem is a nail".

As North American political analyst Andre Korybko puts it, "Unconventional Warfare does not just happen by itself; instead, it is the continuation of an already existing conflict within society, and the role of Unconventional Warfare is to assist the anti-government movement operating within this conflict to overthrow the authorities".[49] According to the aforementioned author, "Unconventional Warfare comprises the second and final pillar of Hybrid War" generally initiated through means of a "Color Revolution" which "in itself is a strategically planted seed to justify the growth of the "democratic liberation struggle". Afterwards, it is succeeded by indirect means and an abundance of more intense psychological mechanisms to reach its objective.

The same author highlighted the document *Special Forces Unconventional Warfare*, of the US military, also known as "TC 18-01", leaked by an informant and published by *NSNBC International* in 2012, as the US manual for conducting hybrid war.

Lawfare employed for geopolitical purposes is a relevant facet of the hybrid warfare model and uses all the resources inherent to it. Laws and legal procedures are used as weapons of war to attack the enemy and to produce results that could be sought in, or lead to, traditional warlike confrontation.

In the US case, this unconventional weapon is facilitated by the exclusive or concomitant use of the *Foreign Corrupt Practices Act* – FCPA – a US law adopted in order to expand the jurisdiction of the US into other countries. In fact, any link with the US, from the use of US currency to any servers located there, among other connections as we will see below, is sufficient to justify action by US authorities in other countries. This clearly demonstrates lawfare with geopolitical purposes.

It follows then that hybrid wars and lawfare have a close relationship, with the latter being an important instrument for the former.

49 KORYBKO, Andrew. *Guerras Híbridas*: das revoluções coloridas aos golpes. São Paulo: Expressão Popular, 2018, p. 71.

2 Strategic dimensions

According to the readings of John Comaroff, contemporary lawfare, similar to conventional wars, consists of three strategic dimensions: *geography*, *weaponry* and *externalities*.[1]

We will examine each of these dimensions in order to understand the integral meaning and scope of the concept.

2.1 The first dimension: geography

Geography is strategic knowledge, and in the words of Yves Lacoste, "the purpose of geography is primarily to make war".[2]

In war, camps and battlefields are chosen in light of their advantages and disadvantages in fighting the enemy. The armed forces strategically use cartography, terrain and geography. Sun Tzu, in his classic work *The art of war*, had already in the fourth century BC, pointed to the importance of geography in strategic calculations; he asserted that "We are not fit to lead an army on the march unless we are familiar with the face of the country".[3]

The geographical option is consequently decisive in the success of a battle or war, and in Sun Tzu's words, is "*a preamble to victory*".[4]

Similarly, David Galula maintains that the role of geography is of utmost importance in conventional wars and of even greater importance in revolutionary wars. The author argues that geography if not favouring those who initiate the battle, can condemn them to failure before the confrontation

---

1 John Comaroff explains lawfare. Retrieved from: www.youtube.com/watch?v=skCRo-tOT1Lg. Accessed 3 September 2019.
2 LACOSTE, Yves. *A geografia*: isso serve, em primeiro lugar, para fazer a guerra. 19th ed. Campinas: Papirus, 2012, p. 27.
3 TZU, Sun. *A arte da guerra*. 24th ed. Rio de Janeiro: Record, 2001, p. 92.
4 TZU, Sun. *A arte da guerra*. 24th ed. Rio de Janeiro: Record, 2001, p. 55.

even begins. As he says, "Geography can weaken the strongest political regime, or strengthen the weakest one".[5]

In the domains of lawfare, the choice of battlefield is equally relevant. The battlefield here is represented by *the public bodies responsible for applying the law*, depending on their respective interpretations of which weapons would exercise more or less force.

The "Prosecutorial guidelines for cases of concurrent jurisdiction: Making the decision – Which jurisdiction should prosecute?"[6] bluntly recommends that the Public Prosecutor's Office seeks a jurisdiction where there is a greater likelihood of conviction. The manual reads: "Prosecutors must identify all jurisdictions where there is a legal basis for potential prosecutions, but also where there is a realistic prospect of successfully securing a conviction".[7]

It is always useful to remember some main procedural guarantees. They include the *principle of natural justice*, in its double aspect, the *prohibition of courts of exception* – as articulated in Art. 5, inc. XXXVII of the Federal Constitution:[8] "there will be no exceptional judge or court". The other is the *guarantee of competent judgement* – in accordance with the principles of Art. 5, inc. LIII of the Federal Constitution: "No one shall be prosecuted or sentenced without the intervention of a competent authority".

International Human Rights treaties ratified by Brazil also include explicit provisions guaranteeing natural justice. Some examples include Article 14.1 of the International Pact on Civil and Political Rights (Decree no. 592/1992) and Article 8.1 of the American Convention on Human Rights (Decree no. 678/1992):

IPCPR
Article 14.1. All persons shall be equal before the courts and tribunals. In the determination of any criminal charge against him, or of his rights and obligations in a suit at law, everyone shall be entitled to a fair and public hearing by a competent, independent and impartial tribunal established by law.

---

5 GALULA, David. *Counterinsurgency warfare:* Theory and practice. London: Praeger Security International, 2006, pp. 23–24.
6 Published by the International Association of Prosecutors.
7 "Prosecutorial guidelines for cases of concurrent jurisdiction: Making the decision – which jurisdiction should prosecute". *International Association of Prosecutors*. Retrieved from: www.iap-association.org/IAP/media/IAP-Folder/IAP_Guidelines_Cases_of_Concurrent_Jurisdiction_FINAL.pdf.
8 N. of T.: National Constitution of the Federal Republic of Brazil.

ACHR

Article 8.1. Every person has the right to a hearing, with due guarantees and within a reasonable time, by a competent, independent, and impartial tribunal, previously established by law, in the substantiation of any accusation of a criminal nature made against him or for the determination of his rights and obligations of a civil, labor, fiscal, or any other nature.

Unfortunately, as we will see, the rules of competition are frequently manipulated or subverted in order to facilitate the use of and to manipulate the weapon. In other words, legal norms are used in legal warfare.

Brazil, as it is subject to the principle of natural justice, repeatedly breaches it via examples of the first dimension of lawfare. We will turn to this subject in due course.

2.2 The second dimension: weaponry

The second dimension of war concerns the weapons with which combatants engage. It is said one must select the most appropriate weapon for any given adversary.

According to David Galula, the choice of weaponry is one of the key challenges in battle. The quantity, the type of arms and the equipment available set limits around the expansion of the insurgents' regular forces.[9]

As regards lawfare, *the weapon is represented by the normative act selected to violate the chosen enemy or by the legal norm improperly selected by the legal text's interpreter.* The most frequently used legal instruments by lawfare practitioners include those of anti-corruption, anti-terrorism and those related to national security. This occurs because such laws, in principle, *contain vague, easily manipulated concepts, allowing for violent precautionary and investigative measures, thus seriously damaging the enemy's image.*[10]

A more complex species of lawfare is used for commercial and geopolitical purposes and is carried out via transnational mechanisms of persecution. One such mechanism includes the *Foreign Corrupt Practices Act* (FCPA), which is a US law originally designed to penalize companies that committed acts of corruption abroad. Currently it is used to provide the US with worldwide jurisdiction.

---

9 GALULA, David. *Counterinsurgency warfare:* Theory and practice. London: Praeger Security International, 2006, p. 35.
10 The enemy's fragile image naturally favours the third dimension of lawfare.

This topic will be explained further below. In continuation, however, companies and businessmen around the world are penalized and forced to pay large amounts to US coffers; as they are accused – with the assistance of local authorities – of violating the FCPA based on radical interpretations of the law.[11] There are also collateral effects of these actions by US bodies working with local authorities, which lead to favourable commercial agreements with companies or sectors of the given country. An illustrative example is the recent involvement of the company Embraer with Boeing, a strategic US company.[12]

In 2016, a series of Brazilian companies like Embraer were persecuted by the US Department of Justice. This resulted in agreements signed with the Department of Justice and the cooperation of Brazilian authorities. These agreements established pecuniary obligations among others, including internal monitoring of the company. A short time later, Embraer was acquired by Boeing. At the very least, it is difficult to believe that only commercial alignments led to this result.

2.2.1 Foreign Corrupt Practices Act FCPA

The strategic use of the law acquires a particular notoriety as a weapon with devastating potential for the economy, politics and geopolitics; drawing from an unmerited conceptual and extraterritorial extension of legal jurisdiction aimed at "combatting" corruption.

The necessity of confronting corruption is obvious, but only within the framework of the rule of law through procedures compliant with due process, in which the impartiality and independence of the judiciary and the judge are respected.

The previously mentioned *Foreign Corrupt Practices Act* (FCPA) 1977, forms part of US legislation that regulates the commercialization of transferable securities.[13] It was modified for the first time in 1988 when it introduced the standard of "knowledge" in the search of legal violations. It added the concepts of "conscious breach" and "deliberate blindness",

---

11 Mike Koehler, in an interesting article, explains that the FCPA is used without any judicial oversight by the US Department of Justice, to impose sanctions on companies in diverse countries, based on very debatable interpretations and legal tenets. KOEHLER, Mike. "The facade of FCPA enforcement". *Georgetown Journal of International Law*, vol. 41, no. 4, 2010.

12 Diario *Valor*. Embraer faz acordos de US$206 milhões com autoridades de Brasil e EUA. Retrieved from: www.valor.com.br/node/4754063.

13 The *Securities Exchange Act*, dating to 1934.

among others, which gave it a broader and more subjective character in interpreting violations.

The second modification of this legislation took place via the 1998 International Anti-Corruption Act. This rule sought to confer an extraterritorial character on the FCPA in accordance with the OECD's Anticorruption Convention model. Henceforth, it extended the FCPA's reach beyond US borders.

A long while ago there were warnings about the perverse effects that anti-corruption laws could have on the geopolitical and business worlds, given such broad concepts and extraterritoriality. The US FCPA is without a doubt the greatest example. As early as 2009, Professor Andrew Brady Spalding described how, from the point of view of political science and economics, anti-corruption laws meant *de facto* economic sanctions on developing countries.[14]

In 2011, the New York City Bar Association[15] warned about the negative consequences that could result from the indiscriminate use of FCPA, especially for business transactions in the country, namely: (i) increasing the cost of transactions (i.e., increased necessity for auditing); (ii) post-transaction integration costs (i.e., adding *compliance procedures* to acquired companies that were not subject to the FCPA standards before); (iii) increased risk of exposure to *enforcement* and the correlated costs (i.e., internal investigations and the payment of fines) and (iv) as a result of the above described and other effects of the FCPA, the abandoning and discontinuing of transactions that, under other conditions, would have been carried out successfully. The New York Bar Association also cautioned in the same document that the excessive use of this legislation has a negative impact on the competition of US and foreign companies subject to the FCPA.

It should be noted that in 2010, both the Department of Justice (DOJ) and the Securities and Exchange Commission (SEC) had already announced their plan to expand the scope of the jurisdiction and implementation of the FCPA; as signalled in an article by Andrew Weissman and Alixandra Smith.[16]

---

14 SPALDING, Andrew Brady. "Unwitting sanctions: Understanding anti-bribery legislation as economic sanctions against emerging markets". *Florida Law Review*, 2009.

15 NY City Bar Association. *The FCPA and its Impact on International Business Transactions – Should anything be done to minimize consequences on the US's unique position on combating offshore corruption?* December 2011.

16 WEISSMAN, Andrew; SMITH, Alixandra. "Restoring balance, proposed amendments to Foreign Corrupt Practices Act. US". *The FCPA blog,* 2011. Retrieved from: https://instituteforlegalreform.com/research/restoring-balance-proposed-amendments-to-the-foreign-corrupt-practices-act/.

Thus until 2010, the FCPA dominated international anti-corruption monitoring. At that stage, other countries began to introduce more extensive and stronger legislation, as is the case with the 2010 UK Bribery Act. The International Organization for Standardization introduced an international standard for an anti-corruption management system in 2016. In recent years, cooperation in enforcement between countries has increased.

This legislation can be subdivided into two parts, namely: (i) anti-corruption measures and (ii) the failures of internal monitoring that affect the accounting and records of a company. The first prohibits the following entities from the action described below: US companies (publicly traded or not) and their officials; American citizens; foreign companies with transferable securities traded on the stock market within US territory or that for any reason have an obligation to submit reports to the SEC or any other person in the United States. The action prohibited is to (a) pay, offer to pay, promise to pay or authorize the payment of money, gifts or any valuables; (b) to a foreign government official; (c) to receive or obtain business.

Since 2016, the year termed the Golden Age of the FCPA, dozens of companies – some of them Brazilian – have formalized agreements with the DOJ and/or SEC because of FCPA enforcement operations, namely:

2016

1. Anheuser Busch InBev
2. Akamai Technologies
3. Analogic, BK Medical ApS and Lars Frost
4. AstraZeneca
5. Bahn, Ban and Harris
6. Embraer
7. General Cable
8. CSK
9. Heon Cheol Chi
10. JP Morgan Securities
11. Johnson Controls
12. Key Energy
13. LATAM Airlines, LAN Airlines and Ignacio Cueto Plaza
14. Las Vegas Sands
15. Mexico Aviation Cases
16. Nordion and Mikhail Gourevitch
17. Nortek
18. Novartis
19. NuSkin

20. Och-Ziff
21. Odebrecht and Braskem
22. Olympus
23. PTC
24. PTC and Yu Kai Yuan
25. Qualcomm
26. Rolls-Royce
27. SciClone Pharmaceuticals
28. Teva Pharmaceuticals
29. VimpelCom
30. Jun Ping Zhang

2017

1. Halliburton
2. Mondelĕz Internacional
3. Ng Lap Seng
4. Orthofix
5. PDVSA Procurement Prosecutions: Hernandez, Ardila, and Beech
6. Sociedade Química and Minera de Chile
7. Mahmound Thiam
8. Joseph Baptiste
9. Halliburton
10. Heon Cheol Chi
11. Patrick C.P. Ho
12. Keppel Offshore & Marine Ltd
13. Ng Lap seng
14. Orthofix
15. SBM
16. Sociedad Química y Minera de Chile
17. Colin Steven (Embraer)
18. Mahmoud Thiam
19. Telia Company AB
20. Zimmer Biomet

2018

1. Beam Inc.
2. Credit Suisse
3. Dun & Bradstreet
4. Elbit Imaging Limited
5. Kinross Gold
6. Koolman and Parker

7. Panasonic
8. PDVSA Procurement Prosecutions
9. Petrobras
10. Eberhard Reichert-Siemens
11. Sanofi
12. Société Générale and Legg Mason
13. Stryker
14. Transport Logistics International and Mark Lambert
15. United Technologies

Orde F. Kittrie cities as an example of commercial and political lawfare what took place at the Siemens company between 2006 and 2008.[17] As we detail in the final chapter of this work, after refusing to comply with a trade embargo between the United States and Iran, Siemens became the target of investigative procedures within the scope of the FCPA in several countries, which resulted in billions in fines and compensation. Regardless of whether the company admitted to improper practices, the motivation of the investigations according to the author had to do with the US attempting to impose external pressure on Iran as part of US geopolitical interests.

2.2.2 The complementary character of the FCPA and FISA weapons

Approved by the US Congress in 1978, the *Foreign Intelligence Surveillance Act* – FISA – was initially restricted to electronic and telecommunication surveillance. However, over time, it underwent various modifications and recently, in the 1990s, its remit was extended to allow physical requisites tied to security investigations, as well as to allow requests for access to phone and email records.

After the fateful terrorist attack on 11 September 2001, the government surveillance body under the FISA empire was increased and the limits of the law were also altered under the Patriot Act.

Whereas before the objective of any FISA investigation had been to collect foreign intelligence information, under the Patriot Act, FISA could be applied to situations in which collecting foreign intelligence was only one of the significant objectives of the investigation. There was no clarification as to what such "significant" objectives might be.

---

17 KITTRIE Orde R. "Lawfare and U.S. national security". *Case Western Reserve Journal of International Law*, vol. 43, 2010.

This lack of delineation allowed for the FISA to be utilized in all types of criminal investigations, whether international or not. Moreover, generic wire taps were allowed without it being necessary to specify what type of device, be it telephone or electronic, or the object of the surveillance. This introduced the possibility that any citizen, American or not, could be spied upon.

But it is not just that. The law passed after the 11 September attacks also eliminated the requirement – from the original FISA text – that the target of surveillance is a foreign agent, for authorization to access telephone records. Consequently, the US government was permitted to access the records of any investigation to gather foreign intelligence information, regardless of proving what the objective of the investigation would be, and their relationship with the other countries that might be deemed possible enemies of the United States.

In 2007 a new modification was made to the initial FISA text allowing US authorities to obtain information about people located outside the US, with a validity of six months.

Even if the Patriot Act was initially temporary, it has been repeatedly renewed over the years not only by President George W. Bush who introduced it, but also by Democratic President Barack Obama. It was effective until 2015 when it was replaced by the USA Freedom Act.

The greatest problem caused by the FISA is that it has been used by the US to monitor potential commercial rivals, and not necessarily to monitor threats to national security, even if we consider the FISA Court to be a secret court. Indeed, both businessmen and foreign politicians – and now, especially the Chinese – prosecuted in the US have reported alleged abuses by the FISA Court.

In a recent article in the journal *Global Investigations Review*,[18] Clara Hudson asks: "DOJ Focus on China 'Is this a weaponizing of the FCPA?'" Since assuming power, former US President Donald Trump initiated an offensive that some specialists have identified as lawfare against Chinese companies. The *"China Initiative"* announced by US Attorney General Rod Rosenstein, promised to concentrate the aggressiveness of the FCPA weapon on Chinese companies that competed with US companies.

US intelligence agencies classified Chinese companies like *ZTE* and *Huawei* as a threat to US national security. On 18 December 2018 DOJ attorneys in cooperation with Canada, arrested the Financial Director of Huawei.

China's defensive strategy which took into account known DOJ practices, included adopting a law – the *International Criminal Judicial Assistance Law* – which prohibited any kind of cooperation, formal or informal, of

---

18 Retrieved from: https://globalinvestigationsreview.com/just-anti-corruption/doj-focus-china-weaponising-of-the-fcpa.

Chinese citizens and companies with foreign authorities. The law strictly prohibits any attempt to disclose Chinese information to foreign authorities that is not authorized by the Chinese government. Once again, the strategic use of the law in commercial and geopolitical lawfare is clear.

According to the previously referenced article in *Global Investigations Review*, FISA has been used to monitor executives of Chinese companies; for example, Mr Ho of the *China Energy Fund Committee*, a company founded by an oil and energy conglomerate called CEFC China Energy.

Mr Ho's investigation is not the only one that seems to demonstrate an overlap with American commercial, geopolitical and national security interests. The way in which FISA is utilized as a weapon for commercial and geopolitical warfare becomes evident.

2.2.3 The context of legislating anti-corruption laws

With the FCPA, the United States developed the idea that US companies would be commercially disadvantaged in relation to foreign companies if legal preventions were not put in place to bar any type of offer, promise or payment giving undue advantage to foreign public officials.

When we started from this premise at the official level, the United States modified the FCPA in 1988 and initiated an international movement the following year to punish the practice of bribery in other countries. The Organisation for Economic Co-operation and Development (OECD, a multilateral organization composed of 37 countries and led by the United States), took decisive action to achieve that goal.

The first step was to create, in 1999, an *ad hoc* working group within the OECD to discuss the issue. Next, it presented research from economists that measured the impact of the bribery of public officials on countries' development and economies. During the Clinton administration as of 1993, the United States sought to reinforce this idea via its training of various US government bodies which could be involved in either the application of FCPA or in the analysis of bribery practices abroad.

Cohen and Papalaskaris observed the following:

> indisputably the most prominent feature of art. 1 is that, although there are two sides to a bribe, the Convention focuses exclusively on the "supply side" or on the providers of bribes, and does not regulate the behavior on the "demand side" or those receiving bribes.[19]

19 COHEN, Paul H.; PAPALASKARIS, Angela M. *International corruption*. 2nd ed. London: Sweet & Maxwell, 2018, pp. 76–77.

In other words, for the OECD, the supply side is the most effective in combatting bribery. In addition, the Convention sought to expand the concept of a "public official". According to the Convention, a "foreign public official" means:

> any individual that holds a legislative, administrative or legal office in a foreign country, whether appointed or elected; any individual exercising a public role in a foreign country, including representing a public company; and finally, any official or representative of an international public organization.
>
> (Art. 1, 4, "a")

According to the same international legal norm,

> "any action or omission of the official in performance of their official functions" includes any use of the office of the public official, whether or not it falls within the "legal competencies of the official".
>
> (Art. 1, 4, "c")

The OECD established a working group to implement the Convention through legislative measures in member countries, and in other countries that agreed to adhere to the multilateral instrument. In Brazil the Convention was promulgated via Decree no. 3,678, of 30 November 2000.

The FCPA system and the OECD Anti-Bribery Convention are, indisputably, relevant instruments when it comes to international efforts in combatting corruption.

However, these legal norms allow for powerful weapons of political, geopolitical and commercial lawfare. Through the Convention, the OECD manages to introduce legislation among the member countries that agreed to the aforementioned norms, broad concepts regarding the concept of a public official and moreover, specific obligations in combatting corruption including at the international level. Through the FCPA, as we have already explained, the United States manages to amply extend its jurisdiction over other states, under the pretext of some illegal practice involving elements related to US territories (email servers, currency, subsidiaries, etc.).

Unfortunately, this critical view of the current reality does not seem to be taken into consideration. Various countries comply with American interference without critique, whether that consists of cooperation with US bodies (especially the DOJ and SEC) in applying the FCPA, or in modifying respective laws and jurisprudence based on the OECD Convention.

Brazil is a very clear example of this. The country modified its legislation regarding anti-corruption after the promulgation of the Convention on Anti-Bribery of Foreign Public Officials in International Commercial

Transactions in 2000, under the government of former President Fernando Henrique Cardoso.

However, the most extensive modifications in Brazilian anti-corruption legislation were made under the governments of former Presidents Lula and Roussef. The apex of this movement was the promulgation of Law no. 12,850/2013 under the Roussef government, which incorporated organized crime and obstruction of justice. It became possible to conduct cooperation or plea agreements and highly invasive methods like surveillance and espionage.

Let us examine the crime of obstruction of justice. Article 2, § 1, of Law no. 12,850/13 says that it is such a crime when anyone "prevents, or in any way hinders, the investigation of a criminal offense involving a criminal organization". This demonstrates how vague the concept now is – and therefore, incompatible with the strict legality that should be applied in criminal law. However, this law is used to justify preventative detention, condemnation of the accused, and even to compel individuals to enter into plea agreements, with the intention of corroborating an accusation. These plea agreements lose their legal weight when, as procured via this sole provision within Law no. 12,850/13 (Art. 4), they have been used by prosecuting bodies (Police and Public Ministry) to supersede any lack of evidence proving the guilt of the accused parties or of planned targets.

In that context, it can be said that currently, Law no. 12,850/13 has become the largest weapon used to practice lawfare in Brazil.

Notwithstanding this emphasis on Law no. 12,850/13, other legal instruments are also frequently employed in the practice of lawfare. In this sense, we could reference strategic use of the law and legal procedures related to *impeachment*. That situation – typically indicative of lawfare – has drawn the attention of some Ministers of the Federal Supreme Court.[20] In a 29 October 2019 session, the Second Chamber of the Federal Supreme Court, when hearing case no. 33,391/CE, of Minister Cármen Lúcia, Minister Gilmar Mendes when providing his vote expressed concern with the growing number of cases in his chamber relating to *impeachment* at the municipal level. On that occasion, Mendes stressed that the issue merited further analysis to determine if the law and the procedures relating to impeachment were being strategically used in order to obtain a political advantage.

Along these lines, there is also the possible strategic use of the *Ficha Limpa* Act [Clean Record Law] (Complementary Law no. 135/2010). In fact, since this law prevents those convicted by a judicial body from participating in an electoral contest, its improper use to harm the candidacy of a political adversary should not be ruled out.

---

20 Official title: Supremo Tribunal Federal.

It is useful to remember by way of illustration, that the lawfare employed against former President Lula also involved strategic use of the Clean Record Law to prevent him from running in the 2018 Presidential Elections. Through a majority of votes, Minister Edson Fachin[21] of the Supreme Electorla Tribunla (TSE) rejected the registration of Lula's candidacy on the basis of a conviction handed down by Sergio Moro, as judge of the 13th *Vara Federal Criminal de Curitiba* [Federal Criminal Court of First Instance No. 13 of the city of Curitiba]. This was even after the UN Human Rights Committee had issued a precautionary measure to ensure that the former president could participate in the elections.[22]

It can be concluded then, that through the strategic use of the *Ficha Limpa* Act, it is possible to prevent an adversary from participating in elections. The strategic use of the *impeachment* law may result in removing an elected political opponent from power. These are practices that also make up lawfare.

This is thus a brief overview of the second dimension of lawfare. Legal norms that, at first glance, are designed for legitimate ends but are ultimately used as weapons against certain enemies.

2.3 The third dimension: externalities

Externalities in lawfare include techniques of information manipulation to generate a favourable or suitable environment to use legal weapons against an enemy. These are strategies used outside of legal battles to defeat an enemy.

Information is manipulated to disorient the opposition and create an unreal scenario. Information is collected to gain strategic advantage. The presumption of guilt is projected, and the opponent is demonized in front of society and public opinion. The media has become the most effective way to influence the community in this way.

The media are used as an external and auxiliary complement to lawfare; manipulated to create suspicion about a given enemy, to discredit them and to obscure the lack of credibility of various accusations.

Throughout history, psychological operations or propaganda serve as strategists' powerful allies.[23] Currently, this dimension has taken on a more central role and perhaps is even becoming more violent.

---

21 Retrieved from: www.conjur.com.br/dl/voto-fachin-registro-lula-tse.pdf.

22 The preliminary measure from the UN Human Rights Committee was obtained by lawyers Valeska Texeira Martins, Cristiano Zanin Martins and Geoffrey Robertson, QC, based on the demonstration that several elements indicated absence of a fair trial in the Lula case.

23 MACDONALD, Scot. *Propaganda and information warfare in the twenty-first century*: Altered images and deception operations. London: Routledge, 2007, p. 1.

In conventional wars of the past, propaganda was transferred by "word of mouth" through rumours. Approximately 500 years ago, with the invention of the printing press, a profound transformation took place. Literacy rates rose as the written word became the dominant method of transmitting information. During World War I, newspapers and magazines reigned supreme in facilitating flows of propaganda or in deceiving the enemy. Only beginning in World War II did images, both in magazines and cinema (although audio also was important) become essential elements of war.

It should be emphasized that in wars, the use of images has always served as a decisive instrument in attacking rulers and politicians, both in order to justify political activities, and to hide and manipulate facts. Scot Macdonald shows us that there are five types of image deception: (i) when a photo or film focuses on certain elements and leaves others out; (ii) when a photo or film contains staging; (iii) when a photo or film is modified; (iv) when the description of the photo or film is altered so that the reader misinterprets it and (v) when there is a photomontage (a combination of several images).[24] It is important to note that the modification of images and *fake news* are not novel phenomena as photographers have been using these techniques since the 19th century.[25]

Susan Sontag has already cautioned the following:

> In the modern way of knowing, there has to be images for something to become "real". For a war, an atrocity, a pandemic … to become a subject of large concern, it has to reach people through the various systems (from the television and the internet to newspapers and magazines) that diffuse photographic images to millions.[26]

In relation to lawfare, the strategic dimension of externalities involves the support provided by the media (or sectors of the media) through various advanced communications techniques. The objective is enhancing strategic use of the law in impacting an enemy. The media creates an environment supposedly legitimizing such persecution by projecting a presumption of guilt on the given enemy (in lieu of presumption of innocence). This is in order to: (i) convict without evidence, or (ii) encourage public opinion

---

24 MACDONALD, Scot. *Propaganda and information warfare in the twenty-first century*: Altered images and deception operations. London: Routledge, 2007, p. 10.
25 MACDONALD, Scot. *Propaganda and information warfare in the twenty-first century*: Altered images and deception operations. London: Routledge, 2007, p. 6.
26 MACDONALD, Scot. *Propaganda and information warfare in the twenty-first century*: Altered images and deception operations. London: Routledge, 2007, p. 6.

to demand a conviction. There is also what is called the *administration of deception*.

In her definition of lawfare, Professor Susan Tiefembrun includes the abuse of externalities and describes it as a weapon designed to destroy the enemy by using, misusing and abusing the legal system and the media in order to create a public outcry against an enemy.[27]

Along these lines, judge Sergio Fernando Moro responsible for the *Lava Jato* Operation in Curitiba, wrote an article entitled "Considerations regarding Operation Mani Pulite".[28] Therein, in light of the Italian experience, he defends the possibility of distorting the law in order to demonize the enemy, beginning with discarding an adversary's presumption of innocence via employing externalities. Moro admitted at the time that it was desirable to exercise the pressure of public opinion on the judiciary and other powers of the republic.

In the article Moro describes the process of delegitimizing targets of judicial operations, seeking sentences without any pushback, and how it can be achieved by repeated negative "leaks" to the detriment of the adversary. A general perception of guilt is constructed using illegitimate means and the selected targets are thus undermined in the court of public opinion.[29] This author suggests, essentially, a trial by media which we will later discuss in further detail.

2.3.1 *The media*

The term "media" is broad and encompasses both international conglomerates as well as online media and blogs.[30] It should be emphasized that its interests and objectives should be to inform. However, especially in large publishing groups, freedom of expression and journalistic integrity is thwarted by editorial interference.[31]

27 TIEFEMBRUN, Susan. "Semiotic definition of lawfare". *Case Western Reserve Journal of International Law*. School of Law, Case Western University, vol. 43, Issue I, 2010, p. 31.
28 MORO, Sergio Fernando. *Considerações sobre a Operação Mani Puliti*. Revista CEJ, pp. 56–62. Brasília, 2004. Retrieved from: www.conjur.com.br/dl/artigo-moro-mani-pulite.pdf.
29 MORO, Sergio Fernando. *Considerações sobre a Operação Mani Puliti*. Revista CEJ, p. 59. Brasília, 2004. Retrieved from: www.conjur.com.br/dl/artigo-moro-mani-pulite.pdf.
30 FENWICH, Helen; PHILLIPSON, Gavin. *Media freedom under the Human Rights Act*. New York: Oxford University Press, 2006, p. 3.
31 FENWICH, Helen; PHILLIPSON, Gavin. *Media freedom under the Human Rights Act*. New York: Oxford University Press, 2006, p. 3.

Jacob Rowbottom alerts us that

> Singling out media institutions as distinct from individual speakers is
> intuitively appealing. However, the appeal of that distinct treatment
> rests on the fact that media institutions generally hold significant com-
> municative power. Focusing on the institutional or commercial nature
> of the large media entity provides a formal criterion that aims to make
> a clean division between media freedom and individual speech, but the
> underlying concern is often with power. That explains why a media
> company that is bankrolled and directed by an oligarch is not a cel-
> ebrated example of individual self-expression.[32]

This scholar points out – as Onora O'Neill highlights – that while self-
expression is a particularly important element in freedom of speech, the
approach is different when looking at powerful media conglomerates.
Communication of the powerful can shape and influence, improve and dam-
age both individual lives and democracies.

Jacob Rowbottom concludes that mass media is not only a set of institutions, but also that these institutions are powerful. The author finally asks:
what is meant by media power? A large media conglomerate cannot coerce
people into doing something they do not want to.[33] In reality, as Manuel
Castells argues, communication is a form of power operating through the
"construction of meaning". In Castells's thought, true power does not lie
in solely convincing people to do things through coercion but can also be
achieved by shaping social meaning. In this way, Jacob Rowbottom posits that the power of media is in shaping public opinion more broadly.
Naturally, this can impact politics as it influences voter decisions on topics
within the political debate. This power has an impact on social life which
influences how others perceive one another.

It is possible in relation to the media, to offer both an *institutional* and
functional definition. The first definition, the institutional, positions the media
virtually as a governmental power alongside the executive, judicial and legislative branches. This definition is fundamental as it deals with the media as
a check among the other powers. The second definition, the functional, is in
contrast with the first as it establishes that media conglomerates indiscriminately have freedom of the press, and all who produce journalistic content can
do so under the cloak of press freedom. However, the crucial point is whether
such freedom, in principle, serves public interests or specific interests.[34]

32 ROWBOTTOM, Jacob. *Media law*. Oxford: Hart, 2018, p. 11
33 ROWBOTTOM, Jacob. *Media law*. Oxford: Hart, 2018, p. 11.
34 ROWBOTTOM, Jacob. *Media law*. Oxford: Hart, 2018, p. 29.

This perspective is key to understanding the difference between concepts of *press freedom* and *freedom of expression*. Freedom of expression centres on the position of the one who expresses, in terms of both the individual self-expression and the autonomy in choosing what is expressed. Freedom of press is justified as a service to the public. This differentiation is necessary as the media are generally institutions holding power, opposed to the common citizen, the latter whose freedom of expression should be protected.

It is an opportune time to re-emphasize the meaning of freedom of expression. In the decision of *James v. Commonwealth of Australia*[35] in 1936, the Judicial Commission of the Privy Council determined the following:

> "Free" in itself is vague and indeterminate. It must take its colour from the context. Compare, for instance, its use in free speech, free love, free dinner and free trade. Free speech does not mean free speech; it means speech hedged in by all the laws against defamation, blasphemy, sedition and so forth; it means freedom governed by law.[36]

In Brazil, for example, radio and television companies provide public services and thus should be subject to the principles applicable in providing such services. Let us assume that a national media conglomerate has signed formal and informal cooperation agreements with a foreign country interested in eliminating a certain competitor and their partners, or a particular politician and their allies. This "cooperation" would already be sufficient basis to question the legitimacy of any news published or omitted for the public. However, as a true public service, with ownership by the Unión Federal [Federal State] as provided for in Article 21, inc. XII, section "a" of the Federal Constitution, all forms of foreign interference in its editorial operations would be forbidden. This is set out explicitly in a section of the FCPA.

Note that freedom of expression and freedom of the press do not come into play with this example, as the very basis of public service is overlapping with and can be questioned by the judiciary.

Other relevant factors in understanding lawfare through campaigns of public deception conducted by companies or media conglomerates relate to interests in certain economic sectors. For example, it could be argued that

35 TROVE. Privy Council. Appeal – *James v. Commonwealth*. Retrieved from: https://trove.n la.gov.au/newspaper/article/25219375.

36 ROBERTSON, Geoffrey; NICOL, Andrew. *Media law*. 5th ed. Thomson: Sweet & Maxwell, 2007, p. 2.

there is a clear conflict of interest in creating a joint venture between a public services provider (sound and image broadcasting in Brazil) and a business conglomerate in the construction sector that seeks to sway the Federal State into aligning corporate and state interests with regard to the oil industry. The media conglomerate's coverage of the country's oil industry would be suspected of serving its own economic interests, and the effectiveness of freedom of expression or freedom of the press over the journalistic content produced would be in question.

In England, the Royal Commission on the Press explained in its Final Report that "Freedom of the press is the degree of liberty or restriction that is essential to allow owners, editors and journalists to promote the public interest through the publication of facts and opinions, without which a democratic electorate cannot judge responsibly".[37]

In this scenario, it should be borne in mind that large media conglomerates may have economic interests in delegitimizing or eliminating the enemy, whether commercial or political. Thus, when discussing the media as an auxiliary to legal warfare (lawfare), this aspect must also be considered in analyzing the whole.

With the development of the internet, instant access to information became available and, at the same time, information was democratized and globalized. Social networks took over a space that was previously solely occupied by TV and print media. Regardless, the responsibility of media conglomerates, internet and social networks remain the same: to inform the public rather than to manipulate it in accordance with corporate interests.

Likewise, with the advent of the internet, a new and problematic form of communication came about. Rumours became a deliberate and involuntary method of propaganda. There is, therefore, a lack of control when it comes to content and its possible distortion. As Shibutani teaches us:[38]

> Content is not viewed as an object to be transmitted, but as something that is shaped, reshaped and reinforced in a succession of communicative acts ... In this sense, a rumor may be regarded as something that is constantly being constructed; when the communicative activity ceases, the rumor no longer exists.

---

37 ROBERTSON, Geoffrey; NICOL, Andrew. *Media law.* 5th ed. Thomson: Sweet & Maxwell, 2007, p. 19.
38 JOWETT, Garth S.; O'DONNELL, Victoria. *Propaganda and persuasion.* 5th ed. Los Angeles: SAGE Publications, 2012, p. 159.

Although rumours can be quickly distributed and disseminated via the internet, they cannot be employed effectively as propaganda. Rumours take on a life of their own and can be turned against those who started them – the propagandists.

In this case, lawfare is adding to the growing pattern of exchanging information via the internet, and campaigning to influence judicial decisions, thus becoming even more destructive. That is why for every lawfare strategist, the internet – based in social networks – becomes an environment conducive to *information warfare.*

As such, there is a direct link to the phenomenon known as *lawfare*, consisting in the use and processing of information to gain a competitive advantage over the opposition. For lawfare, this phenomenon is relevant when it is employed to carry out a disinformation campaign via media interference.

Given this scenario, several countries attempting to ensure good practices by the press created councils to receive and investigate complaints regarding poor or bad journalism. Organizations have been established in recent decades in countries like Ireland, Sweden, the Netherlands, the United Kingdom, Australia, India, Denmark and Finland.

In Denmark, for example, the Press Council created in 1992 under the Local Media Responsibility Law, decides whether a particular publication contradicts press ethics, and whether mass media should be compelled to publish a retraction. According to that law, both content and conduct of mass media must be in accordance with press ethics. Thus, upon the receipt of a complaint, the Council analyzes the arguments contained within and, if applicable, an actor is granted the opportunity to correct the erroneous published information. In turn, the Social Media Council of Finland was created in 1968 by editors and journalists within mass media to establish rules of good conduct in professional practice, defending freedom of expression and freedom of the press. Thus, any person believing that good professional practice has not been upheld by the media can file a complaint before the Council. In a case where a violation is identified, a notice is issued that must be published by the offending party within a short period of time. In certain circumstances, when many important principles are involved, the Council may initiate an investigation and issue statements.

With a view to preserving the justice system, England created the law – *contempt of court*, in which the media is responsible for generating substantial risk in judicial proceedings. The media is not prohibited, but restrictions are set on journalistic coverage of judicial processes or pending prosecution. Its aim is to protect justice, which should always ensure fair, independent and impartial prosecution. Again, any threat to that concept is a threat to both the justice system and rule of law.

For example, if a member of a jury or a judge becomes aware of previous convictions or multiple proceedings existing with regards to a given defendant, it may be deemed prejudicial prejudgment against that individual, divorced from facts and evidence. In addition, any media reports or campaigns used to intimidate judges to obtain certain decisions are increasingly common. These practices compromise the independence of judicial decisions and true investigations. Note that the most important element to be protected is the justice system: its credibility and its independence.

Article X of the Universal Declaration of Human Rights and Article 14 of the UN International Covenant on Civil and Political Rights established that every individual has a right to a fair, independent and impartial trial. But what does this really mean for the independence of the judicial power? Suddenly, judicial independence must be understood as a guarantee of non-interference from the other powers, institutions or political interests in judicial decisions. Above all, the independence of the judiciary from public opinion is important. As Frank Kross notes, "An independent judicial power should not engage in public opinion polling before issuing its sentences". It is precisely the independence of the judiciary that allows for protecting minority rights against potential majority oppression.39 Former US Supreme Court Judge Jackson wrote that the right of a citizen to "life, liberty, property, free speech, freedom of press, freedom of religion, right to assemble and other fundamental rights cannot be put to a vote".40

The independence of the judiciary should never be confused with lack of *accountability* – responsibility of the judiciary. On the contrary, judicial independence does not mean that magistrates can judge by an impulse of ideological persuasion, but rather through legal parameters without need for justification.

A paradigmatic case of undue influence includes a case brought before the European Court of Human Rights, *Worm v. Austria*, of 29 August 1997. In this case, Mr Alfred Worm, an Austrian journalist who worked for the outlet *Profil*, had been convicted by the Vienna Appellate court after publishing an article criticizing Austria's Minister of Finance, Mr Hannes Androsch, while a trial regarding his alleged fiscal evasion was still pending sentencing. Mr Worm was convicted of having unduly influenced the outcome of the Minister's trial. The sentence included a pecuniary fine and

---

39 CROSS, Frank. "Judicial independence". *In*: WHITTINGTON, Keith E.; KELEMEN, Daniel R.; CALDEIRA, Gregory A. (Eds). *The Oxford handbook of law and politics.* Oxford: Oxford University Press, 2008, p. 559.

40 CROSS, Frank. "Judicial independence". *In*: WHITTINGTON, Keith E.; KELEMEN, Daniel R.; CALDEIRA, Gregory A. (Eds). *The Oxford handbook of law and politics.* Oxford: Oxford University Press, 2008, p. 560.

20 days in prison if he did not pay it. According to the Austrian Court, there was no doubt that in relation to the magistrates in the case, reading Mr Worm's work was enough to influence the outcome of Mr Androsch's trial. Mr Worm appealed to the European Commission of Human Rights, alleging that his rights to freedom of expression and information were violated (Article 10 of the European Convention on Human Rights). On 23 May 1996, the Commission acknowledged that a violation of Mr Worm's rights had occurred as per Article 10 of the Convention. Subsequently, a collegial trial by the European Court of Human Rights concluded in a majority decision that Mr Worm's conviction did not violate his right to freedom of expression and information. The conviction was fair and aligned with the Austrian Media Act precepts which provide that:

> Any person who discusses, after the indictment ... and before the trial in the first instance of a criminal proceeding, the probable outcome of those processes or the value of such in a way so as to influence the process' results, will be punished.[41]

The European Court of Human Rights understood that punishing the journalist was done so in protecting the impartiality and independence of the judiciary. In the trial, it was reaffirmed that all human beings have the right to a fair trial, including public figures. In addition, according to this precedent, it is the role of prosecutors and not journalists to establish whether the individual is at fault.

For some time, academia and in the highest regional and international courts have debated the influence or interference of the media in the justice system. How it may prevent a fair trial[42] and what the consequences of media prejudgment and trial by media[43] would be. This is exactly what takes place in lawfare cases in the third strategic dimension, or in other words, in externalities.

In a trial by media, a tactic intrinsic and essential to lawfare includes journalistic coverage of certain accusations or criminal proceedings in which individuals are accused of having committed a crime or irregularities. There are consequences of this stigmatization, not only legally, but also in the

---

41 ECHR. *Worm v. Austria.* (83/1996/702/894). 29 August 1997. Retrieved from: http://hudoc .echr.coe.int/eng?i=001-58087.

42 A *fair trial* is one that is conducted fairly by an independent and impartial judge (free of prejudice), in which the laws are observed both in their material and procedural aspects. In a fair trial, a broad and contradictory defense must take place and those in custody have the right to legal representation.

43 ROWBOTTOM, Jacob. *Media law*. Oxford: Hart, 2018, p. 112.

individuals' professional and personal lives. These joint actions represent a gross violation of the fundamental right to a presumption of innocence. On the other hand, the role of the media is also essential in illicit judicial proceedings, as it can and should expose misconduct of public agents that employ the practice of lawfare. In this regard, it is worth highlighting the historical import of a series of reports published by *The Intercept Brasil* that began on 9 June 2019, in which the strategies and tactics of agents within Operation *Lava Jato* were exposed to the public.[44]

Brazil, sadly, is fertile territory for the publication of false, slanderous and defamatory reports; as a Press Council or any other effective means of fielding complaints regarding illegal conduct by the media has not been instituted. Thus, due sanctions are not applied on those who make a livelihood through slander and defamation. The courts have also not punished press abuses or prevented further incidents of such. At times, the courts have tolerated unlawful acts committed by the press under the pretext of "freedom of the press" – forgetting that the Constitution provides for the right to contest and indemnify material, moral or reputational harm, moral or image (Brazilian Constitution, Article 5, V), and at other times have fixed damages at such low amounts that punishment has no effectiveness and even less of a pedagogical nature.

The position of the Brazilian press has worsened in recent years. There has been a series of media campaigns conducted in favour of political persecution against certain enemies targeted by practitioners of lawfare. Those campaigns, of course, exert a strong influence on society that in turn end up "pressuring" decision makers as they decide, in order to gain popular approval.

Public International Law states that actions of the press, as well as prejudgments of accused public officials, can violate the right to the presumption of innocence. According to the General Commentary 32, Paragraph 30, of the UN Human Rights Committee regarding presumption of innocence highlighted in Article 14 of the International Covenant on Civil and Political Rights, "it is the duty for all public authorities to refrain from prejudging the outcome of a trial, e.g., by abstaining from making public statements affirming the guilt of the accused".[45]

---

44 THE INTERCEPT. *As mensagens secretas da Lava Jato.* Retrieved from: https://theinte rcept.com/series/mensagens-lava-jato/.

45 Translation of the General Commentaries of the UN. Human Rights Treaties of the UN. 2018. Retrieved from: www.defensoria.sp.def.br/dpesp/ repositorio/0/Coment%C3%A 1rios%20Gerais%20da%20ONU.pdf.

In the case of *Gridin v. Russian Federation* heard by the UN Committee in July 2000, it was understood that a public accusation of guilt issued by a high-ranking prosecutor in a public meeting, combined with leaks of this accusation from a hostile press, had violated Article 14 (2) of the Covenant. The Committee affirmed in the case that comments made by the media could harm a fair trial, if the state fails to use its powers to regulate them.[46]

This interference of the press in decisions to be made by public powers, especially the judiciary, perfectly illustrates the third dimension of lawfare – characterized by externalities. Externalities are essentially a series of complex elements that, despite remaining outside of the judicial process, create the ideal environment in which to target an enemy.

2.3.2 Information warfare

As previously mentioned, an essential aspect of lawfare manifests itself in regard to *"information warfare"*. This can be translated as a strategic advantage in accessing and obtaining information from an enemy:[47]

> Coming to grips with information warfare ... is like the effort of the blind men to discover the nature of the elephant: the one who touched its leg called it a tree, another who touched its tail called it a rope, and so on. Manifestations of information warfare are similarly perceived ... [T]aken together all the respectably held definitions of the elephant suggest that there is little that is not information warfare.

Information warfare has become so broad and complex that we could not find a satisfactory definition for the technological dimension of war and lawfare. In fact, information warfare has so many facets that it is difficult to understand.

Megan Burrows describes it as, "a class of techniques, including collection, transport, protection, denial, disturbance and degradation of information, by which one maintains an advantage over one's adversaries".[48] This definition is applicable to all situations in which there is some dispute or competition, whether in the public sphere, as well as the private, commercial, military

---

46 HRC. *Gridin v. Russian Federation*. Retrieved from: https://juris.ohchr.org/Search/Deta ils/378.

47 LIBICKI, Martin C. *What is information warfare?* Washington: National Defense University, 1995, p. 3.

48 BURROWS, Megan. *Information warfare:* What and how? Retrieved from: www.cs.cmu .edu /~burnsm/InfoWarfare.html.

and political spheres. In this technological dimension of lawfare, war over the narrative becomes essential in achieving the objective of harming and delegitimizing an enemy. To explain information warfare, we will examine some techniques and methods utilized in both obtaining and manipulating information.

2.3.2.1 Information gathering

Information gathering translates into an inherent, strategic advantage for the one possessing said information regarding the actions and strategy of their enemy. Precise knowledge of the enemy's next steps allows for disarming and neutralizing their future actions. By way of example, in the Lula case, via monitoring the legal strategies and mobile communications of the defence, the prosecution gained a strategic advantage and tactics over its adversary, the former president. In obtaining this information so as to anticipate the opposing party's action, the opposition could be neutralized by means of counter-narratives in the media, or via legal actions within *Lava Jato* itself.

Lawyers are some of the victims of lawfare, and for this reason, safeguards should be put in place for them, whether in the business, political, geopolitical or military arena.[49]

Information is an offensive strategy that could be within the computer systems or networks of a law firm. This is why protecting the defence from lawfare in the form of cyber-attacks takes on great significance in the information warfare context.

2.3.2.2 Information dissemination

The transfer of information has the same relevance and can be presented in the same way that information gathering was discussed.

For centuries, generals discussed how to carefully disseminate this information carefully. As a result, there is no one answer regarding the best way to transport the information collected through lawfare. For example, information can be transferred via electronic means, such as email, WhatsApp or telegrams. In any case, the most common method of transport is by simple transfer on hardware, on pen drives and so forth.

It is worth keeping in mind that even when there is a transfer of information in lawfare, it should abide by legal dictums or will be considered a crime.

---

49 LIBICKI, Martin C. *What is information warfare?* Washington: National Defense University, 1995, p. 3.

When it comes to lawfare, and there is an agent offending the state, as in the Lula case, the seriousness of such illegal transfer supersedes.

2.3.2.3 Data protection

Strategic information must always be preserved in lawfare. It is recommended that everyone involved in cases of lawfare in the technological world observe cybersecurity rules, such as firewall installation, file cryptography and passwords. Firms and clients should always protect sensitive information related to a case, especially considering the technological dimension of surveillance that has arisen in recent years. Information is key to a successful lawfare strategy, both if on the offensive or on the defensive.

2.3.2.4 Information manipulation

In the manipulation of information, several technological resources that are now widely accessible can be used to distort files (text, audio, video and images). This manipulation is aligned with strategy initially designed for war and can be employed so as to demonize the enemy, for example. In this regard, Scot Macdonald asserts, "A picture is worth a thousand lies".[50]

The adulteration of images can even result in the modification of historical facts. In his famous work *1984*, George Orwell reminds us:[51]

> It was true that there was no such person as Comrade Ogilvy, but a few lines of print and a couple of faked photographs would soon bring him into existence ... Comrade Ogilvy, who had never existed in the present, now existed in the past, and when once the act of forgery was forgotten, he would exist just as authentically, and upon the same evidence, as Charlemagne or Julius Caesar.

2.3.2.5 The misrepresentation, degradation and denial of information

Information warfare possesses three relevant techniques, namely: (i) disturbance, (ii) degradation of information and (iii) denial of information. They are all aimed at preventing the enemy from comprehensive and

---

50 MACDONALD, Scot. *Propaganda and information warfare in the twenty-first century*: Altered images and deception operations. London: Routledge, 2007, p. 9.

51 ORWELL, George. *1984*. New York: Harcourt, 1977, p. 46.

accurate information access.[52] In universal language they could be termed the following: (i) *spoofing,* (ii) *noise introduction,* (iii) *jamming* and (iv) *overloading.*

Spoofing is a technique used to degrade the quality of information provided to the enemy. For example, the flow of information is interrupted via inserting a spoof or false message. The technique is effective as it causes the enemy to err in strategic decision making. Another way to disrupt communication is inserting noise into the communication frequencies of the enemy, to hinder them or even induce them to make a mistake.

Jamming is the technique by which signals between two communications are intercepted.

Finally, the *overloading* technique involves sending an amount of information that is enough to paralyze or freeze an adversary's system, eventually causing a crash or a severe blow to the ability to obtain data. As such, the system is managing so much information that it is unable to distribute the information to the necessary users. This type of attack is also used in the study of law, so that information is either lost or unusable in a lawfare environment.

2.3.3 Psychological operations: PSYOPS

As we have detailed, information and communication signify power, and guide the strategic anticipation of an adversary's actions. But how can information be used to influence the actions of the enemy, or a large portion of society against the enemy?

PSYOPS are operations designed to transmit information with the intention of influencing emotions, deceptions, actions, rationales and finally, the behaviour of governments, organizations, groups and individuals.

In the context of manipulating information and emotions, *fake news* takes up quite a bit of space, given widely used social networks and social media. It is important to differentiate the two intrinsically linked concepts of misinformation and disinformation. Misinformation is inaccurate or incomplete information that influences public opinion or obscures the truth. Disinformation can also be inaccurate, but it is deliberately aimed and disseminated with malicious intent, with a specific purpose in mind. The main difference is the intention to deceive.[53]

---

52 BURROWS, Megan. *Information warfare:* What and how? p. 3. Retrieved from: www.cs .cmu.edu/~burnsm/InfoWarfare.html.

53 COOKE, Nicole, A. *Fake news and alternative facts: Information literacy in post-truth era.* Chicago: LA Editions, 2018, p. 6.

According to Garth S. Jowett and Victoria O'Donnell, propaganda includes reinforcement of cultural myths and stereotypes that are so profoundly interconnected and revealing, it is not a very simple task:[54]

> Propaganda is the deliberate, systematic attempt to shape perceptions, manipulate cognitions, and direct behavior to achieve a response that furthers the desired intent of the propogandist. Its systematic nature requires longitudinal study of its progress. Because the essence of propaganda is its deliberateness of purpose, considerable investigation is required to find out what the purpose is.

Propaganda is a tool that can be used positively or negatively, and is utilized most effectively via entertainment, education and persuasion. The element of entertainment attracts an audience, while the educational aspect distracts from the realization that it is propaganda.[55]

Scot Macdonald warns that its recipients are more easily persuaded by credible or seemingly credible sources, especially if such a source is a specialist in the subject. Credibility, however, is only one characteristic of the source.[56]

History demonstrates that the best manner of communicating propaganda is to tell the truth. According to William Daugherty's thought:[57]

> propaganda, truth pays (...). It is a complete delusion to think of the brilliant propogandist as being a professional liar. The brilliant propogandist is the man who tells the truth, or that selection of the truth which is requisite for his purpose, and delivers it in such a way that the recipient does not think that he is receiving any propaganda ... if you give a man the correct information for seven years, he may believe the incorrect information on the first day of the eight year when it is necessary, from your point of view, that he should do so. Your first job is to build the credibility and persuade the enemy to trust you although you are his enemy ... The art of propaganda is not telling lies, but rather

54 JOWETT, Garth S.; O'DONNELL, Victoria. *Propaganda and persuasion.* 5th ed. Los Angeles: SAGE Publications, 2012, p. 289.
55 MACDONALD, Scot. *Propaganda and information warfare in the twenty-first century*: Altered images and deception operations. London: Routledge, 2007, p. 32.
56 MACDONALD, Scot. *Propaganda and information warfare in the twenty-first century*: Altered images and deception operations. London: Routledge, 2007, p. 35.
57 DAUGHERTY, William E. *A psychological warfare casebook.* Baltimore: John Hopkins Press, 1958, p. 39.

selecting the truth you require and giving it mixed up with some truths the audience wants to hear.

Finally, in examining the theme, Garth Jowett and Victoria O'Donnell[58] created an interesting methodology composed of ten stages, meant to analyze and identify *PSYOPS* or propaganda. The division of these stages considers the following questions: with what objective, in the context of the time, does an agent of propaganda working through an organization reach an audience via a certain symbol, in order to achieve a desired reaction? Moreover, if there were opposition to propaganda, what form does it take? Finally, how is propaganda successful? The issues are as follows:

1. the ideology and objective behind the propaganda campaign;
2. the context in which the propaganda takes place;
3. identifying the agent of propaganda;
4. the structure of the propagandist organization;
5. the target audience;
6. media techniques used;
7. special techniques used to maximize effects;
8. public reaction to these various techniques;
9. counterpropaganda when it exists;
10. effects and evaluation.

In considering these techniques, note that those most recently used by *Cambridge Analytics* in several elections throughout the world were classified by the British Army as weapons of war. As such, they have been used in both traditional war as well as in legal war, or lawfare.

2.3.3.1 Operations of illusion or deception

It is understood that manipulating information, associated with advanced psychological tactics, always formed part of conventional war and could not be different in the case of legal wars. Another technique or weapon of these psychological techniques in this field is what is called operations of illusion or *deception*.

---

58 JOWETT, Garth S.; O'DONNELL, Victoria. *Propaganda and persuasion*. 5th ed. Los Angeles: SAGE Publications, 2012, p. 290.

Scot Macdonald clarifies that

> *The principles of deception are the science; the application of those principles as stratagems are the art. Regardless of the deception operation, the principles are the same, while the stratagems vary endlessly, only limited by the creativity of the most dishonest and creative minds.*[59]

The word *deception* is rooted in the sense of deceiving or creating an illusion. However, in an information war, the objective is not solely to deceive the adversary. The goal is to cause the enemy to understand reality differently. Karl Von Clausewitz teaches that "A great part of the information obtained in war is contradictory, a still greater part is false, and by far the greatest part is somewhat doubtful". Therefore, when conducting a *deception operation* it becomes necessary to establish a series of tactics: (i) that the enemy needs to act and execute (rather than think); (ii) an objective (making a decision); (iii) a story (what is understood as the objective); (iv) a plan (how to convey the story to achieve the objective) and (v) occurrence (the parts of the plan for the story to achieve the objective). Scot Macdonald mentions the importance of developing a schedule and scenario in order to gradually provide the opponent with the information. In this way, the enemy will arrive at an incorrect conclusion regarding the situation.[60]

It is understood, therefore, that *deception* (illusion) is based on true information but managed in such a way so that it is understood differently, and that the opponent arrives at the wrong conclusion. James Jesus Angleton, a CIA officer cited by Macdonald, adds "*the essence of disinformation is provocation, not lying*".[61]

The elements discussed in this chapter demonstrate how externalities make the practice of lawfare viable. These externalities include information warfare, psychological operations (PSYOPS) and deception. Externalities seek to manipulate the truth and provoke artificial stimuli in a society, as well as to disorient and discredit the targeted enemy.

59 MACDONALD, Scot. *Propaganda and information warfare in the twenty-first century:* Altered images and deception operations. London: Routledge, 2007, p. 83.
60 MACDONALD, Scot. *Propaganda and information warfare in the twenty-first century:* Altered images and deception operations. London: Routledge, 2007, p. 11.
61 MACDONALD, Scot. *Propaganda and information warfare in the twenty-first century:* Altered images and deception operations. London: Routledge, 2007, p. 83.

3 Tactics

We have already had the opportunity to highlight the indissoluble relationship between strategy and tactics. In this sense, it is now necessary to describe the tactics corresponding to the strategic dimension.

3.1 Classification of tactics

It is worthwhile to keep in mind that tactics are a means of executing strategy, and that in both conventional warfare and lawfare, they must be analyzed as an *interdependent* whole. In this respect, Carl von Clausewitz highlights:[1]

> We propose to consider first the single elements of our subject, then each branch or part, and, last of all, the whole, in all its relations – therefore to advance from the simple to the complex. But it is necessary for us to commence with a glance at the nature of the whole, because it is particularly necessary that in the consideration of any of the parts their relation to the whole should be kept constantly in view.

Likewise, it seems useful to define certain tactics, grouped according to their corresponding strategic dimension, instead of simply providing examples of tactics adopted in relevant cases of lawfare. We do not of course propose we will exhaust all categories of tactics but rather present those that are representative of the various domains of lawfare.

Instead of classification – which is an exhaustive selection of the reality – this typology allows for recognizing an open and incomplete reality,

1 CLAUSEWITZ, Carl von. "O que é a guerra?" *In: Da guerra.* 3rd ed. São Paulo: Martins Fontes, 2014, pp. 7–30.

compatible with the heterogeneity and dynamism of tactics.[2] In other words, the conceptual permeability of typological thinking is appropriate in examining lawfare tactics.

3.2 Tactics corresponding to the first strategic dimension

As explained above, in war, both camps and battlefields are carefully chosen based on strategic advantages and disadvantages. In lawfare, strategic and tactical choice are of equal import. The battlefield in this context is represented by a jurisdictional, administrative or political body[3] which is responsible for applying the law. The choice of the specific body can be decisive in lawfare's success, provided that the accusation or legal thesis has more or less force depending on who is charged with judging the matter.

3.2.1 Forum shopping

In the legal field we encounter so-called forum shopping; the choice of the forum or jurisdiction where a claim will be presented. In this practice, the objective is to choose both the law (weapon) and jurisdiction (geography) that is most favourable. Note that this choice, or shopping, must be made among relevant jurisdictions.

Regarding this matter, Fredie Didier teaches us:[4]

It is completely natural that, given the existence of various forums, an actor chooses the one he considers most favorable in defending his interests. It is undoubtably part of the same. The problem arises when reconciling the exercise of this right with good faith. This choice is not immune to the prohibition of abusing such a right, which is essentially exercising a right in contradiction with good faith. It is true that the principle of good faith is valid in procedural law, which holds that abuse of the law is illicit. It is also true that due process of law imposes an appropriate procedure, which among its other components, takes place within a jurisdiction. The requirement of adequate jurisdiction is a corollary to the principles of due process, admissibility and good faith. You can even talk about the principle of proper jurisdiction.

---

2 VALIM, Rafael. *A subvenção no Direito Administrativo brasileiro*. São Paulo: Editora Contracorrente, 2015, pp. 41–43.

3 In impeachment cases, rulers are judged via congresses or parliaments, which are constituted as tribunals. We can cite two paradigmatic cases, including that of former President Dilma Rousseff, and that of King Charles I of England.

4 Retrieved from: www.frediedidier.com.br/editorial/editorial-67/.

In defensive lawfare, many times a change in jurisdiction is essential. Retreating from a geographical field where there is certainty of defeat due to a partial magistrate, for example, is a tactic that can neutralize an attack.

At the same time, it is important to underline that in a defensive strategy of forum shopping, the rules of competition must be observed. This is to avoid another principle that prevents abusive forum shopping, which is *forum non conveniens*. According to this doctrine, the judge can reject the jurisdiction based on different criteria, some of them too subjective.

For Beat Walter Rechsteiner there are limitations in applying the concept of *forum non conveniens*:[5]

> In the first place, there must be a different forum from the one in which the process was originally established, which turns out to be an equal jurisdiction in which to consider the litigation. This forum should be the most convenient for the parties. To evaluate the criterion of convenience, one must analyze private interests regarding the litigation in the specific case. Among others, relevant private interests of the parties include: access to the evidence (primarily immovable goods), where the witnesses are coming from, the implementation of the sentence and the procedural costs. On the other hand, those elements that are irrelevant include application of a right that favors one of the parties, or the fact that another legal system does not correspond to that jurisdiction, in a way so that fundamental rights are guaranteed to all parties in the process, as provided for in the domestic legal system. If the private interests of the actor or defendant do not prevail, the court will subsequently examine the doctrine of *forum non conveniens* from the perspective of the relevant public interest. In this sense, it could be that the court is not familiar with the applicable law of the given case. Finally, the most convenient forum (*forum conveniens*) should address claims made within its legal system with adequate sanctions correspondent to the power of the forum so that there is no potential that the actor is denied justice in a foreign jurisdiction.

The fact is that even with correct and impartial application of the concept, there is a tendency to maintain those jurisdictions and forums chosen by the actors. This is especially so in lawfare operations where externalities act to artificially maintain the jurisdiction selected by its strategies, as is further explained in the following.

---

5 RECHSTEINER, Beat Walter. *Direito Internacional Privado*: teoria e prática. 18th ed. São Paulo: Editora Saraiva, 2016, pp. 274–275.

3.2.2 The manipulation of jurisdictions

For some lawfare strategists, victory is only possible if the war is waged in a certain jurisdiction, outside of which there would be no potential for success. In those cases, when bad faith is employed, or in other words, there is an abuse of legal norms and established principles such as natural justice or impartiality, manipulation of jurisdictional rules occurs.

Several factors should be included in choosing strategy: (i) a partial judge; (ii) partial prosecutors; (iii) tendentious and partial hierarchy in submitting claims; (iv) historical, cultural and socioeconomic context of the jurisdiction; (v) relationship between those responsible for applying the law in a certain region with foreign agents, most notably in the case of geopolitical lawfare.

In the context of Operation *Lava Jato*, for example, with unfortunate frequency, people investigated for facts that took place in a specific jurisdiction have been illegally prosecuted and judged by judges who have been proved incompetent (i.e., without jurisdiction or authority over the case, as per the applicable norms).

The series of reports published in June 2019 by the outlet *The Intercept*, provides details about coordinated action between the Federal Public Ministry and former judge Sergio Moro. It signals, among other illegal occurrences, the concern regarding how he maintained the accused within his jurisdiction. In effect, Moro considered himself the only one capable of "prosecuting and sentencing the powerful", including former president Lula, who was always treated as if he were the enemy by the former judge and members of Operation *Lava Jato*.

Later we will see the same tactic utilized in the case of Senator Ted Stevens, in which prosecutors deliberately pressured that the jurisdiction be the Washington courts, despite the facts and the people involved being in Alaska. This was because Stevens was highly approved of in Alaska, including by members of the local justice system, which would hinder implementing externalities, all of which pertained to *information warfare*.[6]

Such behaviour can easily be traced to the first dimension of lawfare. In order to impact the enemy, a battlefield is chosen for its favourable conditions in which to manipulate the law, in accordance with the plan of attack, leading directly to obtaining convictions without evidence.

---

6 However, it is important to note that in the Stevens case, the tactic was not successful, as all the narratives highlight the independence and impartiality of the judge conducting the trial.

3.2.3 Libel tourism

Another tactic linked to geography, and encompassed in the concept of forum shopping, includes the practice of defaming. Not in the jurisdiction where an offence occurred, but in courts that are accepting of the accusation, and would not require proof regarding the accused. This situation has been termed by prominent lawyer Geoffrey Robertson as *libel tourism*.[7]

In courts where *libel tourism* is practised, the defendant is charged with proving their own innocence. Susan Tiefenbrun notes that British courts are known for operating in this manner, unlike, for example, US courts.[8]

3.3 Tactics corresponding to the second strategic dimension

We will now examine tactics pertaining to the second strategic dimension, which include cases that transform legal norms into weapons to harm or destroy enemies.

3.3.1 Frivolous charges or lack of just cause

In order to prosecute in the legal field, just cause is necessary (Art. 395, Inc. III, Criminal Procedure Code). This concept has evolved in Brazil alongside the evolution of time and civilization and has been most recently formulated in the Federal Constitution of 1988.

In the original drafting of the Criminal Procedure Code of 1941 (of fascist origins), just cause was configured as all accusations that described an action categorized as crime. With the emergence of the Federal Constitution and an effort to correct authoritarian norms, there was reform of criminal procedure legislation.

The concept currently in force in Brazil holds that beyond the mere description of a fact classified as a crime, it is necessary that some minimal components support the allegations or accusation. It is important to keep in mind the "certainty of presenting a fact of such a nature that it is subsumed into a certain type of crime",[9] alongside concrete indications of the perpetrator of criminal practice. This more modern understanding

---

7 ROBERTSON, Geoffrey; NICOL, Andrew. *Media law*. 5th ed. Thomson: Sweet & Maxwell, 2007, p. 127.
8 TIEFENBRUN, Susan. "Semiotic definition of lawfare". *Case Western Reserve Journal of International Law*, vol. 43, 2010, p. 54.
9 BADARÓ, Gustavo Henrique. *Processo penal*. 4th ed. São Paulo: Revista dos Tribunais, 2016, p. 175.

recognizes the need to avoid unfounded, frivolous or impulsive allegations beyond the powers and obligations of criminal prosecution bodies. It has become necessary because every accusation leaves a tarnish of infamy on the accused, causing a stain on their character by virtue of the mere fact they are involved in a criminal prosecution.

There are clear signs as to the quality of an accusation that may or may not be acknowledged by the prosecuting body. In criminal procedures, "proof of materiality" is necessary as well as "proof of authorship". This means that the accusation should, in presenting a criminal allegation, prove in conformance with the law that the criminal occurrence actually occurred.

The accusation must also be founded in concrete elements that provide, at the very least, some indication that the accused may have committed the crimes described in the accusation. This is what the law refers to as proof of probable cause. A test of probability that the defendant has already committed the actions defined as illegal, at the time of the accusation.

Accusations without materiality or without just cause are lawfare *instruments* par excellence, from which the most varied weapons (i.e legal norms) are utilized against enemies.[10]

3.3.2 Excessive preventative prison as a form of torture to obtain cooperation agreements

Prisons, especially those of a preventative nature, should be reserved for specific cases in which there is verification that if the accused were not imprisoned, society or the legal process may be put at risk. What is seen, however, is that the exceptional nature of prison is neglected in Brazil and is rather used as a method of depriving the rights of the accused and forcing them to adopt a position of "cooperator".

Along these lines, one of the pillars of Operation *Lava Jato* has been the use of denunciations or confessions as means to expand the scope of

---

10 The chief prosecutors of the *Lava Jato* Task Force of Curitiba, Deltan Martinazzo Dallagnol, offered a thesis that clearly aims to legitimize the prosecution of criminal actions without conforming to the principles of materiality of probable cause. In the book *As Lógicas das Provas no Processo* (Porto Alegre: Livraria do Advogado, 2015), cited by much of the work presented by the aforementioned *Lava Jato* Task Force, Dallagnol defends that to "prove is to plead" (p. 11). Moreover, he sustained that it would be possible to prove a crime through the "inference of the best explanation" (p. 11). He also affirmed that a crime could be proven in the "absence of an alternative explanation that only the accused could prove" or in the case of the "omission of the person responsible to produce evidence that is easily accessible" (p. 283).

investigations, to rationalize requests for precautionary methods and, ultimately, the condemnation of the chosen enemy.

Lava Jato's path to obtaining infamous collaboration and confessions is almost always the same. A person whose statement would be useful to the legal-political ends of the Task Force is identified; there is a progressive and gradual increase of pressure exerted on this possible collaborator (various investigations are opened, precautionary measures are taken, including preventative detention and investigation of family members or those close to the collaborator); and the maintenance of various precautionary methods in order to stifle the individual under investigation. Hence, they feel "collaboration" is the only manner in which to maintain what is left of their dignity or their assets; or that it is even the only way to free their relatives from similar persecution by these criminal prosecution bodies. Once an agreement is signed, the informer quickly receives benefits and there is a rapid cessation of the investigations and precautionary pressures previously noted.

The use of illegal preventative imprisonment, including imprisonment for months or years without concrete justification, is a form of torture for the accused and potential "collaborators". In the words of Antonio Claudio Mariz de Oliveira, "With *Lava Jato*, another preventative prison emerges, which is prison by connection. This has a small difference in relation with torture: in torture, the person speaks more quickly because they are punished. In preventative prison, it takes a bit longer".[11]

Even with the Task Force's official discourse that prison and precautionary measures have not been intended to force collaboration of their chosen targets, some insincerity occurred. Take the incident in which Sergio Moro ordered, on 15 February 2017, a search warrant for the residences of Apolo Vieira, who was accused of bribery by investigators, and then on 21 February he reconsidered the sentence, justifying doing so due to the fact the accused was "in talks regarding a collaboration agreement".[12] In other words, one day the accused represented a great risk to public order ("They make a profession out of what is illegal and a fraud. Preventative prison is a way to put a stop to their criminal careers, and is necessary")[13] and then on another day, it ceased to be so, as information from the Federal Public

---

11 Retrieved from: https://veja.abril.com.br/politica/mariz-prisao-preventiva-para-obter-delacao-e-pior-que-tortura/.
12 Retrieved from: www.conjur.com.br/2017-fev-23/moro-ordena-prisao-recua-saber-acusado-negocia-delacao.
13 Resolution of Sergio Moro 15 February 2017. Retrieved from: www.conjur.com.br/dl/moro-ordena-prisao-empresario-volta.pdf.

Ministry informed, "there would be talks regarding a collaboration agreement with Apolo Santana Vieira".[14]

Messages of prosecutors in the application *Telegram*, discovered in a series of reports titled "*Vaza Jato*",[15] also prove what we are asserting. As an example, it is possible to find in these disclosed messages that there was a series of coordinated actions aimed at pressuring Raul Schmidt, the subject of bribery allegations, made up of precautionary measures taken against his daughter.[16] Once the planned search warrant had been procured, in the words of Nathalie Schmidt's defence, "three Federal Police officers with machine guns violently entered the individual's [Nathalie's] residence and yelled at her to reveal her father's whereabouts, threatening she should 'avoid headaches for her son' [Nathalie's son, a minor of seven years at the time]".

Another illustrative example revealed by "*Vaza Jato*" is with respect to the accused Bernardo Freiburghaus, who was also allegedly involved in bribery. In the conversation, Deltan Dallagnol, leader of the *Lava Jato* Task Force in Curitiba, proposed: "I think we have to block his assets, accounts and real estate in Switzerland. Go there and tell him he will lose everything. *Bring him to his knees asking for surrender*. There is no way for him not to take it".[17]

For these reasons, preventative prison in *Lava Jato* has always been equated with torture, not just by lawyers and jurists, but also by Federal Supreme Court justices like Gilmar Mendes.[18] It is a powerful weapon, which when used indiscriminately and abusively mortally wounds the *spontaneity* of the collaboration, an essential legal element. It also contaminates all evidence obtained from the "confessions", as has been known for centuries, an individual being tortured will say anything to stop it.

3.3.3 Using extracted confessions or cooperation agreements to delegitimize and annihilate enemies via false incrimination

Corruption has become one of the most frequently discussed problems in research in recent years and constitutes an inarguable phenomenon about

---

14 Resolution of Sergio Moro 21 February 2017. Retrieved from: www.conjur.com.br/dl/ moro-ordena-prisao-empresario-volta1.pdf.

15 Name of text: It can be translated as "car wash leaks".

16 Retrieved from: https://theintercept.com/2019/09/10/moro-devassa-filha-investigado/.

17 Retrieved from: https://noticias.uol.com.br/politica/ultimas-noticias/2019/08/29/dalla gnol-vazou-informacoes-de-investigacoes-para-imprensa-aponta-dialogo.htm?.

18 STF, Habeas Corpus n. 166.373/PR, Rel. Min. Edson Fachin. Retrieved from: www.conjur .com.br/dl/leia-voto-gilmar-ordem-alegacoes-finais.pdf.

which there is little debate. On both the left and the right, everyone is against corruption and in favour of measures that seek to confront it.

However, as laws against corruption have evolved, it has been demonstrated that forced confession has become a sure path to social and criminal conviction of people allegedly involved in acts of corruption.

Such confessions should be analyzed with extreme caution. Firstly, the practice of "seizure" of assets is a very fragile "proof" in the criminal process, as it encourages the informant to say anything in exchange for an advantage. Secondly, from the perspective of *carrots and sticks*, the institution of confessions or informants is easily degraded in a quest to condemn an enemy. Therefore, confessions or informants are an optimal lawfare tactic by which to attack an individual undergoing the criminal process and to obtain their sentencing, especially when you have already determined the enemy.

From the moment an authority negotiates an individual's rights with the expectation of receiving information about an alleged immoral practice done by the individual, the situation is configured so that the individual is *blackmailed into informing* and it is not a *spontaneous denouncement*. Even worse, the authority may decide not to abide by the deal if the narrative they receive was not supportive of the objective they were seeking.

This form of operating was strategically used extensively throughout the *Lava Jato* operation, principally on the eve of elections, as happened in the case of Paulo Roberto Costa, former director of Petrobras, in 2014. He was imprisoned and given the right to house arrest in exchange for reporting others involved in the case in which he was a suspect. There is also the unfortunate episode of the denouncement obtained from Antonio Palocci, former Minister of Finance briefly after the 2018 election, so that public opinion would judge and condemn the accused.

As such, Otto Kirchheimer instructs us:[19]

> the defendants admitted to what was a prefabricated and alternative reality. The prosecution put up a collection of motley facts in which real occurrences were inextricably bound up with purely fictitious happenings. But their admixture pointed to an alternative reality.

Otto Kirchheimer himself warns that to achieve such an alternative reality, that is to say, statements about facts that are not true, strategies of lawfare use "techniques of translation":[20]

---

19 KIRCHHEIMER, Otto. *Political justice*: The use of legal procedure for political ends. Princeton: Princeton University Press, 1961, p. 117.

20 KIRCHHEIMER, Otto. *Political justice*: The use of legal procedure for political ends. Princeton: Princeton University Press, 1961, p. 108.

To obtain the alternative reality, the proceedings followed what have been called "rules of translation" (...). They took the defendants through the remotest possible situations that could arise from what they made them admit were consequences of their political action. They always forced on them interpretations that were in line with the prosecution's theory of how the defendants would have acted had these situations arisen. The difficulty of the prosecution's enterprise was that proof rested more or less exclusively on the confessions of defendants and testimony of codefendants, but without any independent corroboration by witnesses outside the scope of the prosecution's power.

This dynamic of arriving at confessional agreements, with conditions attached (forcing the accused to give up their rights and declare prepared statements) to achieve eventual benefits – and with them media visibility if a defendant is convicted – is a true inquisition against enemies declared by the state. People are made guilty overnight based on words that are often debatable and misunderstood.

It is observed, therefore, that forced statements, depending on the circumstances, can constitute a powerful weapon by which to delegitimize, harm or annihilate an enemy.

3.3.4 *Overcharging*

In the criminal process, the prosecution can use *overcharging* as a tactic to ensure incrimination of the accused. Criminal law doctrine, both Brazilian and international,[21] defines excess charging in two ways: vertical and horizontal. Vertical excess occurs when the level of an accusation is increased to a graver state than what actually happened. For example, when an increase in penalty is sought that does not align with the facts. Horizontal excess, in turn, refers to including several facts in one incident. For example, a plurality of behaviours.

It is at this point, when fear of criminal conviction is considered, that overcharging becomes a primary tactic of prosecutors in order to force the accused to accept a "less burdensome" situation in the criminal process. Prosecutors set the bar with an excessive accusation and then set up a "negotiation" to come up with the correct or lesser accusations against the accused, giving the defence the impression that they achieved some type of victory.

---

21 LIPPKE, Richard L. *The ethics of plea bargaining.* Oxford: Oxford University Press, 2011, p. 31.

In the United States, mainly in applying the FCPA, it is very common to see this excess of charging in cases where the DOJ obtains a *plea bargain*; that is, an agreement in which the accused pleads guilty to an accusation in exchange for obtaining benefits. Prosecutors accuse an individual or a company of violating the law and threaten the accused with loss of property, involving family members in the alleged crime and receiving a harsh prison sentence. By this logic, the accused accepts a predefined agreement, supposedly less harsh, to be rid of the sentence corresponding to the facts initially alleged in the accusatory hypothesis.

The US justice system has a high rate of such agreements. They make up approximately 90% of agreements in criminal cases.[22] However, this type of agreement can deprive the accused of rights, since he does not bring the accusations before an impartial judge and ends up complying with the accusation.

Brazilian prosecutors have imported this tactic so as to obtain statements or confessions. This is demonstrated most clearly in Operation *Lava Jato*, especially after the series of reports from the outlet *The Intercept Brasil* entitled "*Vaza Jato*". Therein the *modus operandi* of the Republic's prosecutors, as well as the judge of the case, were revealed. The use of excess accusations or overcharging in various cases became evident. The most emblematic examples are related to cases with compounded charges (corruption and money laundering) for a single act (horizontal overcharging) and allegations based solely on the word of informants.

Matheus Agacci describes what happens to the informants and accused when under pressure from the criminal prosecution very well:[23]

> On occasion, the businessman, is charged in a criminal proceeding, and psychologically affected by the situation, fearing preventative prison, threatened without legal basis and via coercive actions, pressured about losing property, with close friends scared of associating for fear of *labeling approach*, with accusations made against family members, under the watchful eye of an oppressive media that publicly anticipates a still uncertain and unproven guilt by calling him a criminal. He is offered the possibility of obtaining benefits if he denounces third parties, to

---

22 FRAGOSO, Rodrigo. *Overcharging*: a prática de exagerar nas acusações. Retrieved from: www.infomoney.com.br/colunistas/crimes-financeiros/overcharging-a-pratica-de-exagerar-nas-acusacoes/.

23 AGACCI, Matheus. *O overcharging no processo penal brasileiro*. Retrieved from: www.migalhas.com.br/dePeso/16,MI311225,31047-O+overcharging+no+processo+penal+brasileiro.

escape from all the pressure he experiences. He accepts, even if the facts need to be invented or embellished upon.

Finally, it is concluded that accusations without just cause and *overcharging* exist more than we had imagined in the criminal process. It should be kept in mind that, if abuses of law occur in the case of public individuals, they must also take place with those in a more vulnerable situation, without media visibility. Therefore, it is up to the defence lawyer to stand up to the excesses and abuses of the law. This is essential to the functioning of justice within democratic states under rule of law.

3.3.5 The carrots and sticks method

The expression *carrots and sticks* is a metaphor for the "punishment and reward" system used to train animals. The US DOJ adopted this method when applying the FCPA to companies, which brought about declarations of guilt and cooperation agreements in exchange for benefits.

In truth, the US DOJ has used the *carrots and sticks* method since 2000. In April 2016, the DOJ announced the launch of a Pilot Project to incentivize companies to declare violations of the FCPA in exchange for benefits, so as to legitimize the methodology of prosecutors. The memo was written by Andrew Weissmann, former head of the fraud session at the DOJ.[24]

In November 2017, Attorney General Rod Rosenstein announced a new policy of corporative *enforcement* of the FCPA, more clearly demonstrating how the *carrots and sticks* approach works in the FCPA-implemented system against companies. The new policy replaced the FCPA's Pilot Program. It maintained some parts of the program but implemented new "incentives" to encourage companies to disclose violations of the FCPA. According to the US prosecutor's manual, the new methodology led to the presumption that the DOJ would cease taking action against companies if they voluntarily disclosed non-compliance to the FCPA, cooperated fully, and took actions to remedy the regulation infraction. That policy, according to the DOJ, would "provide for reduced fines for business organizations that voluntarily disclose criminal conduct, fully cooperate, and accept responsibility for the criminal conduct".[25]

The government's success in applying the FCPA is due to the *carrots and sticks* method, which always gives the impression that the company is being

---

24 Retrieved from: www.justice.gov/archives/opa/ blog-entry/file/838386/download.
25 LUBAN, David J.; O'SULLIVAN, Julie R.; STEWART, David P.; JAIN, Neha. *International and transnational criminal law*. New York: Wolters Kluwer, 2019, p. 621.

compensated instead of being punished severely. The reward, or "carrot", is a supposedly less damaging path for the company because it assumes that even if the law is violated, condemnation and public exposure regarding involvement in corruption is avoided. This is a very lucrative business for the government.

Mike Koehler, an FCPA scholar, asserts that the *carrots and sticks* method used by US authorities to fight corruption demonstrates a fallacy of the FCPA. The defendants accept agreements and declare their guilt in accordance with what the authorities decide. Koehler expresses concern about the dynamics of making agreements entirely outside of the legal ambit. He contends that the judicial process facilitates the presentation of points of view, with the attenuation of facts and circumstances, by allowing the defence to participate in an oppositional process that may guarantee an impartial and fair decision.[26] In another article, Koehler understands that such voluntary disclosures feed a thriving sector revolving around the FCPA. Both the private sector and government have interests in continuing in this way, as it can benefit companies, law firms and the government. Koehler mentions that law enforcement agencies encourage such behaviour because it makes their work less costly. [27]

The greatest problem is that this strategic and aggressive use – at both the local and international level – of this legislation should be subject to constant judicial review, which has not occurred. The transparency of a (legitimate) judicial process, with a counterargument and broad defence, becomes essential to verify accusations. This judicial scrutiny is particularly appropriate in cases when multimillion- and multibillion-dollar corporate penalties and fines are at stake, as is the case with FCPA enforcement procedures.[28]

In the United States, decades ago, within the FCPA context, judicial reviews were practically non-existent. This is because criminal prosecution was substituted by criminal agreements, including *non-prosecution agreements* (NPAs or criminal immunity) from the DOJ; or *deferred prosecution agreements* (DPAs) leniency deals or *plea bargains,* or agreements with the SEC.

---

26 KOEHLER, Mike. "The facade of FCPA enforcement". *Georgetown Journal of International Law*, vol. 41, no. 4, 2010, p. 997. Retrieved from: https://papers.ssrn.com/sol3/papers.cfm?abstract_id=1705517&download=yes.

27 KOEHLER. Mike. "The FCPA under the microscope". *University of Pennsylvania Journal of Business Law,* vol. 15, 2013, p. 16.

28 KOEHLER, Mike. "The facade of FCPA enforcement". *Georgetown Journal of International Law*, vol. 41, no. 4, 2010, p. 909. Retrieved from: https://papers.ssrn.com/sol3/papers.cfm?abstract_id=1705517&download=yes.

In practice, in most cases, the FCPA means exactly what the DOJ and SEC claim it to be; an accusatory theory that goes unchallenged. This characteristic of the FCPA, unfortunately, has carried over to other parts of the world and *Operation Lava Jato* is a lamentable example. In this operation, the same technique of *carrots and sticks* is used with the purpose of obtaining a criminal negotiation without ever proving the criminal accusation. As detailed in the "*Vaza Jato*" scandal, the chief prosecutor argued that people should be brought to their knees in surrender.[29]

In sum, the transnational nature of the FCPA has become "anything goes", "anything that is legally-related", that perfectly serves the *strategization* of the law that lawfare conducts.

3.3.6 Creating obstacles for lawyers fighting against state arbitrariness

According to Scott Horton,[30] lawfare has been used extensively to intimidate and silence lawyers. This is a common tactic employed by authoritarian regimes, which view lawyers as merely an extension of their clients.

A clear example of this lawfare tactic is found in the grave, vulnerable conditions that Guantanamo prisoners face. They are sometimes detained without any evidence as to their alleged crimes and subjected to torture and inhumane treatment.

Government policies incessantly presented a series of obstacles to legally representing prisoners, with the clear intention of weakening the right to a legal defence. In this regard, David Luban argues that the rule prohibiting lawyers from sharing "classified information" with their clients, represented a major obstacle created by the state in establishing trust between a lawyer and their client.[31] It is noteworthy that this "classified information" was regarding simple data, including the reasons for a client's arrest, and other information that was basic and necessary in preparing the defence. Furthermore, prisoner access to telephones was prohibited and the local mail, excessively delayed, was frequently intercepted by public authorities.

Thus, not only were there great and obvious practical difficulties in preparing the defence of the accused, it was also impossible to establish

---

29 Retrieved   from: https://theintercept.com/2019/08/29/lava-jato-vazamentos-imprensa/. Accessed 30 October 2019.

30 HORTON, Scott. "The dangers of lawfare". *Case Western Reserve Journal of International Law*, vol. 43, 2010, p. 168.

31 LUBAN, David. "Lawfare and legal ethics in Guantánamo". *Stanford Law Review*, vol. 60, 2008, p. 1994.

a trusting relationship between lawyer and client, which contributed to the action of lawfare.

This lawfare tactic represented a true affront to Number 16 of the *Basic Principles on the Role of Lawyers*, which states, "Governments shall ensure that lawyers are able to perform all of their professional functions without intimidation, hindrance, harassment or improper interference".

To effectively perform their professional duties, lawyers must not only be protected by the due process as guaranteed in national and international norms, but also be free of pressure from the judiciary, prosecutors and members of the press. Fairly and efficiently administering justice entails that lawyers perform their work without being subjected to any form of intimidation.

According to the General Report by the UN Special Rapporteur on the independence of judges and lawyers in 2016, in the current context it becomes necessary to establish a renewed commitment to the principles of an independent and impartial justice system. In order to ensure that these commitments become a reality, all stakeholders, including political figures, members of the judiciary, prosecutors and civil society representatives must remain aware of the role of lawyers in a democratic society. They should respect and protect their independence, with the understanding that they play a key role in preserving the fundamental rights of citizens.

3.3.7 *Taking legal action in order to silence freedom of expression and instil fear among those who publicly oppose lawfare*

The fear instilled when frivolous lawsuits are filed against activists, writers, politicians and journalists who offer either a critique or satire of arbitrary action conducted in the context of lawfare, has produced profoundly detrimental effects in terms of freedom of expression.

According to Susan Tiefenbrun, this lawfare tactic has achieved considerable success in Canada, as judicial systems and their laws do not offer the same degree of freedom of expression guarantees as provided for in the United States Constitution.[32]

In Brazil, social networkers, journalists and bloggers who have voiced opposition to lawfare have been subject to numerous legal actions brought by members of the justice system. Property has been seized or high fines imposed, seriously harming freedom of expression.[33]

---

32 TIEFENBRUN, Susan. "Semiotic definition of lawfare". *Case Western Reserve Journal of International Law*, vol. 43, 2010, pp. 54–55.
33 Retrieved from: http://midianinja.org/renatamielli/a-censura-no-brasil-veste-toga/.

3.3.8 States of exception (creating ad hoc law)

In exploring the contiguous categories of lawfare, we had the opportunity to elaborate upon the concept of the state of exception and placed it within the tactics of the second dimension of lawfare.

Essentially, if there is no adequate legal norm in force addressing war, it is created *ad hoc*, using the technique of exception. An illustrative – and objectionable – example of this includes the tactic employed within the context of Operation *Lava Jato*, through a sentence put forth by the Federal Regional Tribunal of the Fourth Region, led by the Federal Judge of Second Instance Rómulo Puzzollatti. In the paragraph below, the court acknowledged the possibility of "exceptional treatment":[34]

> ⁘   Now, it is known that criminal proceedings and investigations resulting from the so-called "Operation *Lava Jato*", under the authority of the represented magistrate, constitute a unique and exceptional case in Brazilian Law. Given such conditions, where there are unprecedented situations, generic legislation that applies to common cases does not apply. In this way, in considering that the privacy of telephone communications of those under investigated in the aforementioned operation had to be set aside. This was in order to preserve the operation from successive and notorious attempts at its obstruction, both by those under investigation and with the intention of guaranteeing the future application of criminal law. It is therefore correct to maintain that the secrecy of telephone communications (Constitution, art. 5, XII) can, in exceptional cases, be supplanted for the general interest of the administration of justice and the application of criminal law. In the face of permanent threat to the continuity of the Operation *Lava Jato* investigations, suggestions as to modifications in legislation, are made, without a doubt, in light of an unprecedented situation deserving of exceptional treatment.

This decision clearly and irrefutably enshrined the state of exception, allowing agents of Operation *Lava Jato* to create their own laws, or in the context of lawfare, their own weapons.

---

34 P.A.N. 0003021-32.2016.4.04.8000/RS – Special Court. In this case, it should be remembered that under threat of grave consequences, the renowned Judge of the Federal Court of Second Instance, Rogério Favreto, was the only member of the Special Court of the Fourth Federal Regional Court who voted to open a disciplinary investigation of Federal Judge Sergio Moro.

3.4 Tactics corresponding to the third strategic dimension

We will now analyze tactics that correspond to the third dimension of law-fare, which, as we know, seek to create a favourable or adequate environment in which to use legal weapons against an enemy.

3.4.1 Manipulating a mobilizing cause in order to pursue the enemy

The tactic of manipulating a mobilizing cause via propaganda so as to make a population conscious of the need to destroy an enemy, is a common practice in war scenarios.

David Galula[35] affirms that the insurgent cannot even contemplate fighting a battle unless he has a rallying cry with which to gain followers among a population. However, he stresses that the creation of such a rallying cry is necessary only at the start of a conflict. As war unfolds, the original cause becomes less important.

One of the mobilizing agents or causes that has the greatest impact and the extraordinary ability to gain support, both from the media and the public, is corruption. Anti-corruption laws and their investigation create true media spectacles that undermine the accused and create the perfect lawfare setting.

As João Feres Júnior teaches, it is important to highlight that

> it is via the media that corruption becomes a scandal, that is, through the programming and the framing carried out by the media, together with practices and facts, makes something public and constitutes a product, with narratives, principal characters, and a given name, for example, *Mensalão, Trensalão, Aeroporto de Cláudio* etc. The scandal is a product that the media constructs by using a single narrative, given a proper name, with a myriad of information, statements, stories, documents and legal proceedings submitted by authoritative voices, given that their profession is journalism.[36]

3.4.2 Encouraging public disillusionment: the influence of public opinion and using the law to create negative publicity

The tactic of public disillusionment consists in uniting forces among those involved in the practice of lawfare, to provoke the disillusionment of the population regarding a given enemy.

35 GALULA, David. *Counterinsurgency warfare:* Theory and practice. London: Praeger Security International, 2006, pp. 8–9.
36 FERES JÚNIOR, João; SASSARA; Luna de Oliveira. "Corrupção, escândalos e a cobertura midiática da política". *Novos estudos CEBRAP*, vol. 35, no. 2, p. 208.

Recently, Brazil was condemned by the Inter-American Court of Human Rights for allowing the disclosure of secret recordings of a personal nature. In *Escher et al. v. Brazil*,[37] the tribunal's decision upheld the law that a judge who authorizes wiretapping of an individual's phone may not, for political or any other purpose, "authorize" the release of its transcripts to the media.

Anthropologist John Gledhill argues that the tactic of promoting public disillusionment is selectively utilized in Brazil and was decisive in the process that ultimately resulted in the impeachment of President-elect Dilma Rousseff. Before the *impeachment* vote, Gledhill maintained:[38]

> What we are seeing in Brazil is how selective application of what could be termed "lawfare" promotes a climate of public disillusionment, to the extent that a democratically elected government can be removed from power.

Thus, in creating public disillusionment, those engaging in lawfare count on the support of the public to facilitate attacks on the adversary.

3.4.3 Lawyers as targets in the information war

As already mentioned, there are several techniques employed against lawyers. In the Brazilian case, the creation of "task forces" and the use of artificial intelligence by criminal prosecutors has been confirmed.

In addition to the asymmetry between the state and the investigated or accused, especially in cases of great repercussions, it should be noted that lawyers are also subject to various illegitimate attempts to obtain data and information.

The *American Bar Association* founded a task force to aid its members in protecting themselves from cyber-attacks, describing it in the following terms:[39]

> Lawyers have become "soft targets in the hunt for insider scoops on mergers, patents, and other deals". At the same time, law firms may not only be soft targets, they may also be attractive targets – if they are

---

37 *Escher et al. v. Brazil*, 6 July 2009, Inter-American Court of Human Rights.

38 GLEDHILL, John. *The Brazilian political crisis*. Retrieved from: https://johngledhill.word press.com/2016/03/17/the-brazilian-political-crisis/.

39 RHODES, Jill D.; POLLEY, Vincent I. (Eds). *The ABA cybersecurity handbook*: A resource for attorneys, law firms and business professionals. Chicago: American Bar Association, 2013.

known to have a large corporate client base, an attacker may be drawn to them, like a bee to honey. While the corporate clients themselves may have sophisticated computer security defenses, their law firms' defenses are probably weaker. And once inside a law firm's defenses, the intruder likely has access to all of the firm's client information.

In 2009, the gravity of the situation prompted the US *Federal Bureau of Investigation* to issue an alert that *hackers* were scanning US law firms for confidential information.[40] They used *spear phishing* or *targeted socially engineered email* to break down a network and its technological defences.

In another case, a grave violation of legal practitioners' rights occurred in the city of Alexandria, in the US state of Virginia, at the law firm *Puckett & Faraj*. The firm worked to defend high-ranking military officers accused of war crimes (including a navy officer accused of war crimes in Iraq), and was hacked by the *Anonymous* hackers. In the cyber-attack, legal documents with details of the defence's strategy were leaked, as well as confidential correspondence between clients, the attorneys of other clients and information regarding other cases. Hackers reportedly gained access via Google email accounts, as the firm was not sufficiently diligent in using adequate passwords.

In the information war, ethics do not exist and the smallest of information security precautions cannot be neglected. Lawyers who work with cases of lawfare, as well as those dealing with sensitive cases, are victims of various data breaches, including the theft or loss of portable electronic equipment such as laptops, computers, hard drives, pen drives, backup drives or any other non-encrypted information. More than a third of breaches occur in this manner.

But what happens if information warfare when spying on the defence strategy is conducted within the justice system itself?

The defence team of former President Lula da Silva, two of whom are the authors of this work, was surveilled by the court of Operation *Lava Jato*. One of the founding partners of this study was the principal lawyer in the case and possessed strategic and privileged information regarding the defence. On 20 February 2016, then judge Sergio Moro justified the authorization surveilling this lawyer, with the rationale that they were a known, long-time friend of Lula. Six days later, prosecutors agreed with this rationalization and added that the lawyer had acted on behalf of Lula and his family in other proceedings.

---

40 Retrieved from: https://biglawbusiness.com/fbi-alert-warns-of-criminals-seeking-access -to-law-firm-networks.

Additionally, at the request of the Republic's prosecutors, Moro authorized wiretapping of the main telephone extension of the law firm for 23 days during which, close to 25 lawyers held privileged conversations with hundreds of clients of the firm, including former president Lula. Phone calls of defence strategies were recorded and monitored in real time by police, who reported on the calls and classified them in order of importance. Moro and the prosecutors were fully aware that it was the law firm's landline, as they also followed the conversations in real time. As with any other law firm in the world, each of the monitored calls began with stating the law firm's name, as per regulations. Moro and the prosecutors were also informed by two official letters sent by the telephone company. Regardless, they continued the illegal monitoring.

Approximately three years after this illegal monitoring, messages that were improperly exchanged between Moro and the *Lava Jato* prosecutors via *telegram* –revealed in the outlet *The Intercept Brasil* and other media during the *Vaza Jato* (Car Wash Leaks) scandal – corroborated all suspicions. It was confirmed they had listened to and taken notes regarding all the confidential conversations between the client, Lula, and his lawyers through intercepting cell phone communication. For more than a month (from 19 February to 16 March 2016), the justice officials had coordinated their combined efforts in the processes against Lula, based on illegal surveillance of his legal defence team.

As a result of this illegitimate action, *Lava Jato* agents were able to monitor all of the actions and legal strategy of Lula's lawyers during a fundamental moment in the process, when the Federal Supreme Court decided whether the case would remain with then-judge Sergio Moro.

4 Paradigmatic lawfare case studies

At this point it is important to demonstrate, through paradigmatic cases, the rich and conceptual repertoire that has been imparted throughout this work.

As such, we will analyze two illustrative examples of political lawfare – the Ted Stevens and Lula cases – and another case of corporate and geopolitical lawfare – the Siemens case.

4.1 The Siemens case

One paradigmatic case of commercial and geopolitical lawfare includes the "anti-corruption" operation directed at the Siemens Aktiengesellschaft (AG) company between 2006 and 2008. Orde F. Kittrie identifies how the Siemens company was subjected to lawfare, in relation to the intensification of a trade embargo placed on Iran by the United States in 2006. It is important to emphasize that the dialogue between the United States and Iran is historically and continuously characterized by tensions and countermoves by both parties.[1]

In this sense, Kittrie asserts that the United States initiated two measures against Iran. One, sabotage (through the spread of computer viruses for example), and the other, imposition of sanctions, which were composed of economic and diplomatic restrictions and above all, actions of lawfare. In sum, such sanctions were configured as strategic use of the law to achieve geopolitical, military and commercial objectives. In the words of Kittrie:[2]

> The sanctions imposed on Iran in recent years – through U.N. Security Council resolutions binding under international law and through

---

1 KITTRIE, Orde R. "Lawfare and U.S. national security". *Case Western Reserve Journal of International Law*, vol. 43, p. 405.
2 KITTRIE, Orde R. "Lawfare and U.S. national security". *Case Western Reserve Journal of International Law*, vol. 43, p. 404.

changes to the domestic laws of the U.S., European Union, and others – have been a particularly salient, deliberate, and, in many cases, creative form of lawfare. The sanctions use law as a substitute for traditional military means to advance an operational objective – in this case, halting Iran's illicit nuclear program.

Considering that the sanctions applied within the framework of the UN Security Council were not sufficient in the view of US authorities, other legal means were pursued and designed to thwart Iranian action. According to Kittrie's studies, the United States: (i) promoted strategic business measures at the regional level in the country, which included divestments of pension funds; (ii) pressured, through legal actions, foreign banks that negotiated with Iran and foreign energy companies that supplied refined oil to Iran and (iii) promoted strategic judicial litigation. These strategies targeted figures from large companies, corporations and financial institutions.

It is worth mentioning, albeit briefly, the most relevant information from the Siemens case.

According to the US government, after the 11 September 2001 attacks, its authorities engaged in the intense work of investigating international banking transactions with the intent of discovering money laundering and terrorist financing operations. It was in this context that the DOJ and the SEC (Securities and Exchange Commission) began investigations against Siemens AG, which, as is widely known, is one of the largest companies in the world.

For two years, the German company was the target of countless criminal prosecution procedures always accompanied by accusations in the media, as per the following timeline:[3]

2006

15 November – Prosecutors announce that they raided workplaces and residences of Siemens officials as part of an investigation into suspected diversion of funds. The Siemens company reported that the investigation was directed towards six individuals and an amount of money in double-digit millions of euros.

---

3 *Timeline Siemens battles corruption scandal*, 15 December 2008. Retrieved from: www.reuters.com/article/us-siemens-timeline/timeline-siemens-battles-corruption-scandal-id USTRE4BE4ID20081215.

20 November – Prosecutors confirmed they entered the offices of company President Klaus Kleinfeld, who was considered a potential witness rather than a suspect.

22 November – Munich prosecutors affirm they are investigating the disappearance of about €200 million (US$269.3 million) from Siemens accounts.

23 November – Siemens creates an anti-corruption task force.

11 December – Siemens cuts its reported net profit in 2005/6 by €27 million in light of the situation and hires outsiders to examine its compliance systems and rules.

12 December – Siemens announces that it is looking into more than €420 million of dubious payments. Thomas Ganswindt, who led the Siemens telecoms business, is arrested.

15 December – The anti-corruption watchdog *Transparency International* asks that Siemens leave their organization.

2007

3 January – A German prosecutor declares that Siemens is under investigation for possible abuses of the UN Oil-for-Food Programme in Iraq.

12 January – Munich prosecutors declare that former CFO Heinz-Joachim Neubuerger has been questioned as a suspect in the bribery investigation.

25 January – Chairman Heinrich von Pierer, also a former CEO, resigns from the Siemens committee that examines compliance issues.

2 February – Siemens announces that the US DOJ and the SEC are investigating potential violations of the US law in connection with the corruption scandal.

14 February – Siemens declares that Nuremberg prosecutors have raided offices in Munich, Erlangen and Nuremberg, all linked to the alleged suspicious payments.

27 March – Siemens executive board member Johannes Feldmayer is arrested on charges of breach of trust and is accused of making illegal payments to the head of a workers' association, as part of the Nuremberg investigation. Later, he leaves the company.

19 April – Von Pierer announces his resignation as Chairman but denies any personal responsibility for the case.

25 April – Siemens selects as Chairman corporate governance expert Gerhard Cromme. Klaus Kleinfeld resigns while denying any wrongdoing.

14   May – Two former managers receive suspended sentences for paying illegal bribes to managers at the Italian utility company Enel, to win turbine contracts between 1999 and 2002.

20   May – Siemens appoints pharmaceutical industry executive Peter Loescher as CEO.

4   October – The Munich court fines Siemens €201 million in the corruption case.

2008

24   January – At the annual meeting, the vote to approve the performance of former executives and von Pierer is postponed. Cromme affirms that Siemens has begun talks with the US SEC.

23   April – Erich Reinhardt, chief of the medical technology department, resigns as suspicious activities regarding his business surface.

30   April – Siemens estimates the dubious payments at €1.3 billion.

9   May – Munich prosecutors declare they have not found evidence that would warrant criminal charges against von Pierer, but that he and other former company officials are under investigation for the administrative offence of breaching their corporate supervision obligations.

28   July – A German court decides to fine and suspend the two-year jail sentence of a former Siemens executive in light of his role in setting up slush funds to win contracts.

29   July – Siemens reveals that it plans to claim damages from 11 former top managers for failing to put a halt to illegal practices.

5   November – Siemens says it will pay around €1 billion to settle a deal regarding the bribery allegations.

In this context, on 12 December 2008, the DOJ, SEC, FBI, IRS (*Internal Revenue Service*, the tax authority in the US) and Munich prosecutors announced they had discovered systemic corruption networks at Siemens in violation of the FCPA. At the time, DOJ prosecutors called a press conference to announce they had filed an action against Siemens in relation to alleged corruption schemes throughout Asia, Africa, Europe, the Middle East and Latin America. According to the prosecutors, the investigations revealed that between 2001 and 2007, the company paid bribes totalling $1.36 billion in pursuing international contracts in Argentina, Venezuela, Bangladesh and Iran.

On the same occasion, the FBI Assistant Director of the Washington field office, Joseph Persichini Jr, said that the announcement of the guilty plea entered by "Siemens AG and several of its regional companies reflects the FBI's dedication to enforce the provisions of the Foreign Corrupt Practices

Act. Simply stated, it is a federal crime for U.S. citizens and companies traded on U.S. markets to pay bribes in return for business". He also said that "The FBI will continue to assist its law enforcement partners to ensure that the corporate and business communities are not tarnished with violations of the kind we are presenting here today".[4] The enforcement partners would be foreign enforcement partners.

Note that this investigation began in the United States, and immediately had worldwide repercussions, with a global multiplication of investigations in other countries. All of Siemens was under investigation for violating the US embargo against Iran, which confirms Kittrie's study.

It is important to note that although the alleged Siemens corruption schemes had not occurred in North American territory, nor did Siemens have headquarters in that country, the DOJ claimed partial jurisdiction over the case as the company had been listed on the US stock exchange since 2001. Consequently, it would then be, in principle, subject to the FCPA given the foreign nature of this weapon.

Another matter that deserves attention is that the facts in the indictment were related to bribes and bribery. However, the DOJ's criminal indictment only dealt with violations and irregularities to do with lack of monitoring or failures in the supervision and preservation of information in the accounting, audits and contracts, among other things related to administration and finances of the company, which demonstrates the tactic of vertical and horizontal *overcharging*.

On 15 December 2008, after negotiations with the DOJ and SEC, Siemens, on behalf of three subsidiaries, agreed to plead guilty and pay a fine of approximately US$1.6 billion to US and European authorities. The fines the company agreed to pay amounted to US$450 million to the DOJ and US$350 million to the SEC. Moreover, the agreement entailed that the company pleaded guilty before the Federal Court in Washington. At the time, the Siemens fine was the highest applied in relation to the FCPA as it exceeded the US$33 million mark of an agreement that had been made with the oil company Baker Hughes. In Germany, the prosecutors closed a deal with Siemens and the Munich court that also entailed the company pay US$290 million. In addition, because of the investigations, the company leadership was ousted.

The DOJ agreement levied several penalties on the Siemens company, but as with all agreements within the FCPA's scope, an independent regulator had to be hired to supervise the internal monitoring and corporate governance. As part of this supervision, the company had to disclose to US authorities in a comprehensive and transparent manner, all of its financial, marketing and competitive strategy, among other information.

---

4 Retrieved from: www.justice.gov/archive/opa/pr/2008/December/08-crm-1105.html.

Likewise, the company's agreement with the DOJ only applied to the company as a legal entity and did not guarantee immunity for executives in individual prosecutions. Consequently, in 2011, the DOJ indicted eight former Siemens executives and officials for conspiracy, bribery, forgery of the accounts, tampering with international regulations and fraud on behalf of the company. The indictment detailed that in 1998, executives had promised to pay US$100 million in bribes to secure a US$1 billion contract to manufacture new identification documents in Argentina. According to the DOJ, this scheme did not go through only because of a change in the body in charge at the time. US authorities affirmed that bribery schemes of a similar nature took place in Venezuela, Iraq and Bangladesh. It was the first time that a member of a multinational executive board was prosecuted for FCPA violations.

Andres Truppel, former CFO of Siemens Argentina, was the first of the executives to enter into a plea agreement and plead guilty. In 2015, he admitted to guilt in the Manhattan Federal Court and claimed he played a significant role in the bribery between 1994 and 2007.

Actions taken to indict the Executive Director of Siemens Argentina, Herbert Steffe, were judged inadmissible, as the Manhattan Court judge decided his alleged conduct was not criminal.

A former member of the Siemens board, Uriel Sharef, was accused of participating in a Siemens bribery scheme, involving Argentinian public officials in 2003. This executive was prosecuted both in the United States and in Germany. In the US the process was shelved. In Germany, the Munich court acquitted Sharef in 2014, unconvinced he was associated with the bribery. In 2018, former manager Eberhard Reichert entered into a plea deal and pleaded guilty before the court in Manhattan after being extradited from Croatia to the US.

As corroborated in the reports of Orde Kittrie, the lawfare strategy employed against Siemens was also implemented at a regional level in the US. For example, in 2009, Californian politicians, activists and human rights defenders (among them, Nobel Peace Prize winner Shirin Ebaldi) went before the Los Angeles Metropolitan Transportation Authority to protest a supply contract with Siemens. They argued that the company participated in a *joint venture* with Nokia in 2008 to sell monitoring equipment to the Iranian government that enabled interception of email, phone calls and internet data.

Given the commotion caused by the protest, the spokesperson for the mayor's office in Los Angeles announced[5]:

---

5 LOS ANGELES TIMES. Siemens's Iran Ties Concern MTA. Retrieved from: www.pressr eader.com/usa/los-angeles-times/20090718/281565171758563.

The mayor has been working to ensure that the city divests from any company that does business with Iran. So obviously, any connection with Siemens or any other potential contractor of Iran would be of great concern to the mayor when considering a contract.

It is important to highlight the role of civil society and mediums of information in the lawfare strategy: ordinary citizens are informed of reprehensible acts by the aforementioned companies. In this case, it was alleged state interference from the Iranians in citizen privacy, which would never be viewed favourably in the West. The citizens then acted in a way that used local laws and decision-making power to impose sanctions on given objectives (directly Siemens and indirectly Iran).

It is worth noting the assertion of Hadi Ghaemi, spokesman for the International Campaign for Human Rights in Iran during the time of these events:[6]

> I think the Iranian people inside the country and abroad are extremely concerned that Nokia and Siemens have enabled the Iranian government to carry out the recent crackdown and oppression using their technology. They are hitting back with the call for a boycott.

And so, in January 2010, Siemens publicly announced it would not negotiate new trade agreements with the Iranian government.

Without handing down any judgment regarding illegal acts, or even in relation to the scope of illegal acts presented in the allegation, we observe in congruence with Kittrie, that the *deflagration of investigations in the Siemens case was motivated by clear geopolitical interests*. On the other hand, *vague allegations and typical lawfare tactics* employed by FCPA authorities make it difficult to analyze allegedly corrupt behaviour.

In summary, it is evident in this case that there is a use of legal norms, notoriously those of the FCPA, as weapons to harm those targets that are in opposition to US geopolitical and commercial interests.

4.2 The Ted Stevens case

Another case worthy of our attention includes that of Theodore R. Stevens, a Republican Senator from Alaska (1923–2010). Stevens was a lawyer who had studied at the prestigious Harvard Law School, as well as being a DOJ Attorney General. In the 1960s he defended the native people of Alaska and

---

6 Retrieved from: https://thecuttingedgenews.com/index.php?article=11472.

became known for his land disputes with the government, being elected six times as Senator.

Between 2003 and 2007, Stevens was President *pro tempore* of the Senate, putting him third in the US Presidential line of succession behind the Vice President and Speaker of the House of Representatives. Stevens was well known and respected among Republicans as well as Democrats. He was the Republican Senator with the longest tenure in the Senate. In 2000, he received the Alaskan Citizen of the Century Award.

Stevens was a friend of the owner and CEO of VECO, an oil and field service company in Alaska. On the one hand, VECO was a successful construction firm in Alaska. On the other, its owner Bill Allen was suspected of having made secret political donations to Alaskan politicians via the company. For this reason, in 2006, the FBI began to investigate Allen for alleged corruption and arrived at a "cooperation" agreement.[7] In exchange for his "cooperation", Allen received a reduced prison sentence, sold his company for US$350 million, and guaranteed his children immunity from prosecution.[8] Regarding VECO, the company also received immunity, as it was crucial for its sale. However, prosecutors incorporated a contractual clause into the cooperation agreement called a "kicker", whereby US$70 million of the sale value would be retained by the purchasing company (CH2M Hill) if Allen did not continue to cooperate with the US government.

This clause made sense for the purchasing company in that, if the US government brought charges against VECO, it would inevitably collapse and consequently CH2M Hill would lose hundreds of millions of dollars. In this way, CH2M Hill forced Allen to continue cooperation with the government. In reality, the majority of the time, "cooperating" was a euphemism for testifying according to the script that the government prepared, regardless of the truth or reality of facts. This cooperation is always accompanied by various "incentives".

In the same 2006 period, rumours in the press indicated that the DOJ was positioned to implicate Senator Stevens in this investigation, because of renovations made to his property that would have allegedly cost more than what Stevens and his wife had paid.

In July 2008, after two years of suspicion and many accusations, Stevens was criminally indicted by DOJ prosecutors on the allegation that he had not observed the US Federal Code of Conduct. Prosecutors held a live press

---

7 CARY, Rob. *Not guilty*: The unlawful prosecution of U.S. Senator Ted Stevens. Washington: Thomson Reuters, 2014, pp. 16–17.

8 CARY, Rob. *Not guilty*: The unlawful prosecution of U.S. Senator Ted Stevens. Washington: Thomson Reuters, 2014, p. 197.

conference to announce the criminal accusations towards the Senator,[9] in which they argued that he had received "gifts" for six years without declaring them and "received" renovation of his Alaskan chalet in the total of $200,000 from businessman Bill Allen, owner of the oil company VECO.

In gross violation of the law, in August 2008, a month before the grand jury, the DOJ employed the tactic of refusing to give the defence all the evidence in the case.[10] Defence attorneys insistently requested access, albeit unsuccessfully.

Even without access to the evidence obtained by the prosecution, Stevens's defence managed to prove that his wife was responsible for the renovation payments and that the couple had obtained bank financing for a total value of US$160,000 to pay the costs of the work,[11] and even mortgaged his residence in Washington DC.

However, prosecutors ignored the evidence of innocence submitted by the defence. It was clear that they had already entered into a cooperation agreement with Allen to blame Stevens and secure his sentence.[12] According to Stevens's lawyers, at the start of the investigations, prosecutor Brenda Morris offered a settlement proposal in the following terms: "*he will plead guilty and I guarantee he will not spend one year in prison*".[13] Stevens rejected the deal and repeatedly maintained he had not committed a crime.

The narrative constructed by the prosecutors arrived at its most tense point when they decided to use a message sent from Stevens to Allen. In the message, Stevens explained that the friendship should not be taken into account, and that the renovation should be done in an ethical way. Based on this message, it was asserted that Stevens was trying to cover himself, or "cover his ass". Whilst Persons, the individual who had brought the message to Allen, had testified in Stevens's favour, the message, which was evidently proof of Stevens's innocence, was billed by the prosecution as proof of guilt.

Allen testified to the court that the message was proof of guilt and that Stevens was sending him a veiled message so as to give the operation the

9 CARY, Rob. *Not guilty*: The unlawful prosecution of U.S. Senator Ted Stevens. Washington: Thomson Reuters, 2014, p. 194.
10 CARY, Rob. *Not guilty*: The unlawful prosecution of U.S. Senator Ted Stevens. Washington: Thomson Reuters, 2014, p. 76.
11 CARY, Rob. *Not guilty*: The unlawful prosecution of U.S. Senator Ted Stevens. Washington: Thomson Reuters, 2014, p. 190.
12 CARY, Rob. *Not guilty*: The unlawful prosecution of U.S. Senator Ted Stevens. Washington: Thomson Reuters, 2014, p. 191.
13 CARY, Rob. *Not guilty*: The unlawful prosecution of U.S. Senator Ted Stevens. Washington: Thomson Reuters, 2014, p. 48.

appearance of legality. With a view to reinforcing this assertion, prosecutors took an extremely aggressive position during the trial.

Stevens's defence attorney described the episode accordingly:[14]

> The prosecutors in the Stevens case suggested that a statement of dis-interest was part of a strategy to "cover his butt". Prosecutors advised the jury that the senator was so preoccupied with appearances that he made up a false text just to hide his true intent. In this distorted view of the government, we live in a Wonderland Country where everything means the opposite of what is said: yes means no, up is down, and proof of innocence is proof of guilt.

This situation dragged on in the courts where details were discussed to the point of exhaustion, and the media reported everything in a distorted man-ner. Consequently, in October 2008, a month before the elections, Stevens was convicted of violating the Federal Code of Ethics.

In December 2008, FBI special agent Chad Joy decided to participate in the whistle-blower programme[15] and denounced the conduct of the DOJ prosecutors in the Stevens case. Joy reported that evidence in favour of Stevens's defence had been withheld. The judge in the case, Emmet Gael Sullivan, instructed that prosecutors deliver all evidence and documents from the Stevens case to the court and the defence by 30 January 2009. On that day, the prosecutors provided evidence to the court but refused to pro-vide it to the defence. Consequently, the prosecutors were removed from the case and a new team took over. From that moment forward, the new pros-ecution team began to provide the defence with access to the documents and emails in the possession of the previous team. After accessing this vast documentation, the defence found that Bill Allen's declarations about "*cov-ering his ass*" during the trial were created by the old prosecution team.

As recorded in the case documents of the prosecutors, Rocky Williams, one of those coordinating the renovation of Ted Stevens's property, would have stated he understood that Allen would have included the amounts referred to regarding payment of services to VECO; the payment would have also been shared with another company involved in the renovation, "Christensen Builders".

---

14 CARY, Rob. *Not guilty*: The unlawful prosecution of U.S. Senator Ted Stevens. Washington: Thomson Reuters, 2014, p. 215.

15 This US legal term refers to an individual that spontaneously reports information to the authorities about the practice of unlawful acts.

However, according to the documentation presented by prosecutors, the witness had claimed he did not know Stevens had paid for the services.

In fact, it was later revealed that Williams underwent a virtual "*cross-examination*" – that is, a mock interrogation that would have been put forth by the Senator's defence team – where the prosecution discovered his testimony potentially damaging for their purposes and favourable for the defence.

Following this unsatisfactory mock examination, coincidentally, prosecutors became concerned that the witness's health was deteriorating, and during the week of the trial, they unilaterally decided to send him back to Alaska, with the rationale that he needed medical treatment.

Williams never returned to Washington after this episode, and his statement was never included in the process. He died from severe liver disease in December 2008, just three months after the trial.[16]

In April 2009, the Attorney General announced that the trial would be halted, as they found the defence was not provided relevant information during the trial. Judge Sullivan scheduled a hearing to set the conviction aside and in April 2009 Stevens was acquitted.[17] Judge Emmet G. Sullivan also requested an investigation into the prosecution's conduct and into possible corrupt practices by the DOJ. On 14 November 2011, after two years of investigations and revising approximately 128,000 documents, Henry F. Schuelke III (the lawyer appointed by Emmet G. Sullivan) filed a 500-page report in court on the FBI investigation and the actions of DOJ prosecutors. The investigation concluded that corrupt legal practices had taken place during the trial. The report shook the US legal world as it is to date considered a case demonstrating the greatest violation of the Brady Rules, i.e., the State's obligation to present evidence of innocence to the defence (*Brady v. Maryland*, 1963).

Ultimately, in 2010, Stevens, as well as some of his family and friends, died in a plane crash in Alaska. According to former prosecutor Sidney Powell,[18] the Terrain Awareness Warning System that allowed audiovisual detection of the terrain had been "inhibited" or disabled. There was no voice recording from the plane's cabin, and three autopsy tests were performed on the pilot to find a cause for the accident. Nothing was found.

---

16 Retrieved from: www.upi.com/Top_News/2009/01/01/Rocky-Williams-Stevens-case-witness-dies/95861230831328/?st_rec=4828499669200&ur3=1.
17 CARY, Rob. *Not guilty*: The unlawful prosecution of U.S. Senator Ted Stevens. Washington: Thomson Reuters, 2014, pp. 302–321.
18 POWELL, Sidney. *Licensed to lie*: Exposing corruption in the Department of Justice. Dallas: Brown Books, 2014, p. 3.

Approximately six months after the plane crash that killed former Senator Ted Stevens, the DOJ chief prosecutor from the *United States v. Stevens* case, Nicholas Marsh, at 37 years old, committed suicide in his home in New York.

Stevens's lawyer asserted that it was undeniable the Senator's illegal conviction had changed the balance of votes in the Senate and guaranteed more votes for the Democrats. He argued that this imbalance had possibly enabled the passage of *Obamacare*, a legislative project from the Obama government that sought to shape public health in the country.

Similarly, former US prosecutor Sidney Powell, in her book *Licensed to lie*, in which she describes what took place within the DOJ in various cases, claims that the process and conviction that took place in the Stevens case had ruined the Republican Senator's political career.[19] She argued this was a result that the prosecutors were deliberately trying to attain. The former prosecutor denounced the Stevens case as conducted illegally and manufactured to create an imbalance of Republican power in the US Senate. Powell claims that the Stevens case is another example of several criminal prosecutions conducted by a group of high-ranking DOJ prosecutors in the interests of power and politics. They used the judicial apparatus and the state's financial support to destroy the reputation of individuals and companies.

During a session of the US Senate analyzing the Schuelke report, Senator Charles Grassley (R-IA) mused about the strategic manipulation of the law via criminal prosecution, to influence elections:

> In his famous speech titled "The Federal Prosecutor", then-Attorney General, and later Justice Jackson said, "The prosecutor has more control over life, liberty, and reputation than any other person in America … While the prosecutor at his best is one of the most beneficent forces in our society, when he acts from malice or other base motives, he is one of the worst". These are fitting words for today's hearing as we examine the conduct of Justice Department prosecutors in an effort to understand what went wrong in the prosecution of former Senator Ted Stevens. The government's prosecution of Senator Stevens was arguably the highest profile case ever brought by the Justice Department's Washington, D.C.-based Public Integrity Section. It had consequences far beyond the jury's guilty verdict and impacted the Alaska Senate election in 2008. While all criminal cases should be handled with the utmost professionalism, cases of this level of importance and publicity

19 POWELL, Sidney. *Licensed to lie*: Exposing corruption in the Department of Justice. Dallas: Brown Books, 2014, pp. 4–10.

– where elections can be swayed – should be shining examples of the best of the Justice Department. They should have the best prosecutors and the best agents, and should be a centerpiece of the American criminal justice system.

This case clearly demonstrates the strategic use of the law to harm an enemy. Prosecutors chose the jurisdiction of Washington DC, even though all the facts of the case and the persons involved pertained to the state of Alaska. The legislation chosen related to corruption and ethics, a preferred weapon of lawfare, as the mere suspicion of corruption is sufficient to alienate allies, isolating the enemy from their troops on the battlefield. Third, externalities were employed extensively through the media, which exhaustively reported any suspicions and discussions regarding the case.

In any case, it is curious to note that in this instance, everything else highlights the impartial behaviour of the magistrate in charge of the trial, which allowed for the subsequent acquittal of the US Senator.

As in the Lula case, Stevens's prosecution employed the same multidimensional strategies and tactics of legal warfare, that is, lawfare. It is also important to emphasize the similarities between the cases; the strategies behind the accusations, as well as the almost identical nature of the facts, which will be further elaborated upon in the chapter on the Lula case.

Finally, and unfortunately, when analyzing Senator Ted Stevens's case, especially via internet research, it is notable that the first results include news related to the Senator's investigation and conviction. The news regarding his acquittal is scarce, relegated to the background in comparison to coverage of the investigation. The importance that the media attributed to the case, even within the investigation, determined the Senator's guilt. Even after the acquittal, he was considered guilty by US society, which demonstrates the violence behind misuse of the law, as it assassinates reputations.

4.3 The Lula case

The judicial siege carried out against former President Lula in the so-called *Lava Jato* Operation represents one of the clearest examples of the practice of lawfare for political, geopolitical and commercial ends.

In the first place, it is evident that a favourable jurisdiction was chosen based on artificial criteria. Indeed, it was not by chance that the 13th Federal Criminal Court of the city of Curitiba, where federal judge Sergio Moro presided, is where the main investigation against Lula originated, as well as his subsequent criminal convictions that eventually led to his imprisonment.

Paraná state shares a 450-kilometre border with Paraguay and Argentina, as well as a border with three other states. The triple border has received particular attention from the United States with the justification of fighting terrorism and criminal organizations. Since the 1990s, the States have directly intervened in the region. In this way, they share information and knowledge from their intelligence services as well as training and recruiting public and private agents.

American agent training extends to judges and prosecutors. Wikileaks has revealed confidential governmental and company documents for the public interest. They reveal, for example, in 2009 in the city of Rio de Janeiro, a course was held for judges and prosecutors in Brazil and Latin America. One of the participants in that gathering included former federal judge Sergio Fernando Moro, as registered in the WikiLeaks database:[20]

> Judge Sergio Moro then discussed the 15 most common issues he sees in money laundering cases in the Brazilian Courts. U.S. presenters discussed various aspects regarding the investigation and prosecution of illicit finance and money laundering cases, including formal and informal international cooperation, asset forfeiture, methods of proof, pyramid schemes, plea bargaining, use of direct examination as a tool, and suggestions on how to deal with Non-Governmental Organizations (NGOs) suspected of being used for illicit financing.

Moro also maintained close contact with US authorities during the period in which he participated in the ENCLA (the National Strategy to Combat Corruption and Money Laundering), a project created during the Lula government and involving various national and foreign authorities. Various federal regulatory and criminal prosecution entities, as well as foreign entities including the OECD (Organisation for Economic Development) participated in ENCLA.

As we mentioned, it is an undisputed fact that the US National Security Agency (NSA) spied on Petrobas and dozens of Brazilian authorities in the upper levels of the Republic. This espionage was made public in 2013 thanks to information revealed by Edward Snowden. In other words, it can be concluded that the US collected data from Brazil via espionage, and after going through it without any established or known criteria, delivered this material to Brazilian prosecutors on the *Lava Jato* Task Force by "informal cooperation". Given US prosecutors' celebration the day the first sentence was

20 Retrieved from: https://wikileaks.org/plusd/cables/09BRASILIA1282_a.html. Accessed 28 September 2019.

issued against Lula, and as verified by videos of the judicial processes, it can also be concluded that the former president's persecution was one of the conditions in exchange for US "informal cooperation" and assistance in the "construction" of the case, as described at the time by authorities.

Within this context former judge Sergio Moro, whom the US authorities knew, as demonstrated above, came on the scene in the investigations and processes against Lula.

It is necessary to digress at this point to clarify that Brazilian legislation outlines criteria for the establishment or modification of a jurisdiction – that is, the space within the power of each jurisdictional body in the country. As a rule, the crime takes place within the jurisdiction of the judge or court (Article 69 of the Criminal Procedure Code). However, out of all the *Lava Jato* accusations the Paraná state directed against Lula, none of the facts took place in Curitiba. The Federal Supreme Court, in a loose interpretation of the law, established in September 2015 (Order on the Issue Summary no. 4,130) that investigations and action related to Petrobas should take place in Federal Criminal Court no. 13. However, there was never any real proof that Petrobas money had been directed towards Lula, as we have always affirmed in documentation throughout the processes. Former judge Sergio Moro himself, when judging the final appeal filed in the "triplex case" (an appeal for clarification of the sentence), recognized that this was the case.[21]

Nonetheless, Moro agreed to preside over the criminal process and to rule on precautionary measures requested by *Lava Jato* of Curitiba against Lula. He went further by acting strongly to maintain this undue jurisdiction through written justifications and manifestly illegal measures, including surveilling lawyers.[22] He also engaged in initiatives that until recently, remained undiscovered, before being revealed by *The Intercept* outlet, among others, in the "*Vaza Jato*" scandal.[23] These publications revealed, among other matters, that: (i) the investigations of Lula were initiated by judge Sergio Moro himself, who requested that Prosecutor Dallagnol listen

---

21 Below is an extract of a judgement issued on 18 July 2017 in the criminal procedure number 5046512-94.2016.4.04.7000/PR ("triplex case") presided over by then judge Sergio Fernando Moro, who was deliberating upon the appeal filed by the defence of former president Luiz Inácio Lula da Silva: "This Court never stated, in a judgment or otherwise, that the amounts that Constructora OAS received from Petrobras, have been used for the former President's undue advantage".

22 Retrieved from: www.conjur.com.br/2016-mar-17/25-advogados-escritorio-defende-lula -foram-grampeados. Accessed 5 October 2019.

23 Retrieved from: https://theintercept.com/series/mensagens-lava-jato/. Accessed 5 October 2019.

to a "source" in order to officially launch these persecutory acts;[24] (ii) the *Lava Jato* Task Force itself was fully aware that it had no real cause to accuse Lula in the "triplex case"; (iii) Moro directed *Lava Jato* prosecutors to attack Lula's defence team over the course of the process;[25] (iv) confidentially, *Lava Jato* prosecutors admitted that Moro violated the "accusatory system" which does not allow the concentration of the functions of accusing and judging;[26] (v) Moro coordinated and guided the Federal Public Ministry's main initiatives against Lula;[27] (vi) the *Lava Jato* prosecutors, without a warrant, accessed fiscal information of those related to Lula.[28]

When put in this light, the first dimension of lawfare was clearly employed in the case. The most favourable jurisdiction was chosen – in the Lula case, truly, a jurisdiction intent on sentencing him.

From the perspective of the second dimension of lawfare, or selecting legal norms to use as weapons, *Lava Jato* decided to investigate and prosecute Lula using the Criminal Organization Law (Law no. 12,850/2013) and legal provisions that deal with corruption (Art. 317 of the Penal Code) and money laundering (Law no. 9,613/99). With this, they sought to obtain the following advantages in the legal war waged against Lula: (i) using plea bargains or cooperation agreements with prisoners or those about to be jailed who, in that state, are willing to declare any kind of narrative in order to avoid torture, whether or not it is true; (ii) employing legal concepts very loosely; (iii) attempting to stigmatize the former president via allegations of highly reprehensible behaviour in the public eye, especially relating to conduct of a politician or a public figure.

Concurrently, there was an intense media campaign launched against Lula, adding the third dimension of lawfare, so-called *externalities*.

In fact, since 2015, the press, as encouraged by members of *Lava Jato*, began to publish allegations and theories of guilt, seeking to link him especially with the illegal acts associated with Petrobas. On 4 March 2016, Lula

---

24 "Não é muito tempo sem operação?" *The Intercept*, 9 June 2019. Retrieved from: https://theintercept.com/2019/06/09/chat-moro-deltan-telegram-lava-jato/. Accessed 29 July 2019.
25 "A Defesa já fez o showzinho dela". *The Intercept*, 14 June 2019. Retrieved from: https://theintercept.com/2019/06/14/sergio-moro-enquanto-julgava-lula-sugeriu-a-lava-jato-emitir-uma-nota-oficial-contra-a-defesa-eles-acataram-e-pautaram-a-imprensa/. Accessed 29 July 2019.
26 "Moro sempre viola o sistema acusatório". *The Intercept*, 29 June 2019. Retrieved from: https://theintercept.com/2019/06/29/chats-violacoes-moro-credibilidade-bolsonaro/. Accessed 29 July 2019.
27 "Não é muito tempo sem operação?" *The Intercept*, 9 June 2019. Retrieved from: https://theintercept.com/2019/06/09/chat-moro-deltan-telegram-lava-jato/. Accessed 29 July 2019.
28 "Olhada Informal" *The Intercept*, 18 August 2019. Retrieved from: https://theintercept.com/2019/08/18/lava-jato-dados-sigilosos-chefe-coaf/. Accessed 29 July 2019.

was subjected to preventative detention,[29] among other cautionary measures. The episode, which was heavily photographed and followed by the media, clearly intended to create an artificial aura of guilt surrounding Lula. The former president was taken by Federal Police to his residence in São Bernardo do Campo in a patrol car, in order to give a statement in the hall of Congonhas Airport in São Paulo.

Subsequently, one of the crudest attacks of persecution directed at Lula took place: a collective convening of and presentation by prosecutors on the *Lava Jato* Task Force, via *PowerPoint*, on the same day as the indictment of Lula in the Curitiba jurisdiction. The *PowerPoint* contained various arrows pointing towards Lula at the centre, as the "mastermind" of a criminal organization. As we demonstrated in presenting the defence, this public display is incompatible with the constitutional guarantee to presumption of innocence, which can only be superseded if the conviction has exhausted its appeals. The Brazilian prosecutors on the *Lava Jato* Task Force of Paraná state did not even have the jurisdiction to charge Lula. Those charges pertained to a specific investigation in progress in the Federal Supreme Court, at the bidding of the Attorney General of the Republic, as would be acknowledged in a book authored by the Attorney General at the time.[30]

29 The pre-trial detention was declared unconstitutional by investigators from the Federal Supreme Court in ADPF judgements 395 and 444, of 14 June 2018 [an ADPF, or *Arguição de Descumprimento de Preceito Fundamental*, is a resource against the actions of public powers that breach a constitutional precept in the 1988 Federal Constitution, similar to Argentina's "recurso de inaplicabilidad de ley" which verifies or corrects errors of the law in a judgement].

30 Brazil's Former Attorney General Rodrigo Janot described the events in the following way in the book *Nothing less than you want* (JANOT, Rodrigo. *Nada menos que tudo: bastidores da operação que colocou o sistema político em xeque*. São Paulo: Planeta, 2019, p. 182 and following): "In September 2016, shortly after accusing Lula of heading a criminal organization, being passively corrupt and laundering money, Deltan Dallagnol asked for a meeting with me in Brasilia. He came with other prosecutors from the Task Force, including Januário Paludo, Roberson Pozzobon, Antônio Carlos Welter and Júlio Carlos Motta Noronha. When they came into my room, I said to myself: Here comes a problem. Every time they came as a group, rather than one or two, it meant something serious. And this time was no different. Dallagnol and his colleagues had come to demand I change my workflow. They wanted me to immediately denounce former President Lula for criminal organization, and to put other charges that were further along in the process on the back burner. At the moment, I had four charges to present: two against the PMDB (one in the Chamber, another in the Senate), one against the PT and another against the PP (...)

'We need you to reverse the order of charges and put the PT charge first', Dallagnol said as soon as the meeting began.

(...)

In other words, according to any perspective, it is clear that the media spectacle conducted by Deltan Dallagnol and other prosecutors of the Republic, alongside the PowerPoint presentation, should never have taken place. But it was important in the lawfare conducted against Lula, since it

---

'No, I am not going to change the order. I am going to follow my criteria, those charges that are further along in the process. There is no reason for me to change the order. Why should I do this?' I replied.

Paludo then said that I would have to prosecute the PT (Worker's Party) and Lula quickly, because if I did not, the complaint they filed against the former President for passive corruption and money laundering would be discovered. By law, an accusation of money laundering depends on an antecedent crime, in this case a criminal organization. So, for them to be able to file before Judge Sergio Moro in Curitiba, I would have to prosecute the former president and other PT politicians in the Supreme Federal Court in Brasilia first. This would be the necessary legal basis to accuse Lula of money laundering.

'Without your own charge, we will forfeit our accusation of money laundering', the attorney said.

The situation was delicate. In the initial phase of investigations into Lula and the triplex, I had asked Minister Teori Zavascki to share with the Task Force documents that we had obtained in our summary of PT criminal organization. They had asked me to access the material and I promptly provided it. In the sentence, the minister clearly allowed that they use the documents, but stipulated that they could not be used for accusations of criminal organization, because the material was already an object of prosecution by the Federal Supreme Court, with the investigation led by rapporteur Teori Zavascki and myself.

Now, what does Dallagnol do? Without previously consulting me or my team, he accused Lula of laundering money from a criminal organization he himself directed. Lula was the 'great general', the 'top commander of a criminal organization', as the prosecutor termed it in the meeting condemning the former president, alongside the *PowerPoint* presentation. In the *PowerPoint*, everything pointed to Lula, who was the alleged head of a criminal organization made up of congressmen, senators and other politicians within the jurisdiction of the Federal Supreme Court.

'If you do not prosecute him now, we will not be able to levy the charge of money laundering', Dallagnol reiterated, immediately after Paludo's demonstration.

'I am not going to do that!' I repeated.

'You are trying to interfere with our work!' Dallagnol exclaimed, clearly irritated.

'I do not want to interfere with your work. From the looks of it, you are the ones trying to interfere with mine. When sharing the evidence, Minister Teori expressly insisted that you could not investigate and report Lula for heading a criminal organization, as that was under investigation in the Supreme Court. And you did. You disobeyed the minister's order and charged him with criminal organization. I have nothing to do with it', I said.

I was quite upset with Curitiba's direct and veiled pressure on our work and at the time it was time to dot the I's. As I spoke, I showed them a copy of the minister's decision, the same decision that had already been sent to them when we had shared the evidence.

(…)

'It's not my problem, it's your problem. You did this without consulting me, ignoring the instructions of Minister Teori. And now I have to fix your problem? No way am I doing that!' I said".

sought to deprive, from the very start, any presumption of innocence that is guaranteed by the Brazilian Federal Constitution.

Throughout the proceedings against Lula, the prosecution presented no evidence of guilt. Moreover, the proof of his innocence was completely disregarded; even documents proving that 100% of the economic-financial worth of the "triplex" had been transferred by the construction company to a fund managed by the *Caixa Econômica Federal*. Moro prevented any expert or technical process of following the money, as is usually carried out when investigating crimes of a financial nature. Then the judge prevented the admission of any evidence that was favourable to Lula's defence.

In essence, this resulted in Lula's arrest, and his exclusion from candidacy in the 2018 presidential elections, based on this pre-established sentence. Everything that was argued in the communication presented before the UN Committee in July 2016, via petition written by the authors of this book – Cristiano Zanin Martins and Valeska Teixeira Zanin Martins – as well as by Geoffrey Robertson QC, came to pass. It was the first individual petition before this international body by a Brazilian citizen. The Brazilian State dismissed an interim measure granted by the UN Committee on 17 August 2018 and reaffirmed on 10 September 2019, which asserted Lula's right to participate in the 2018 elections until he was allowed a "fair process".

Lula's conviction and imprisonment are linked, on the one hand, to internal political factors. This allowed for the rise and pursuit of a political project that in a different setting would not have achieved such visibility. And the individual largely responsible for Lula's conviction and imprisonment, former judge Sergio Moro, emerged as the key actor in this extravagant political scenario.

On the other hand, Lula's conviction and imprisonment, as well as the wear and tear of the political universe that revolved around the former President, allowed for Petrobas and consequently all of its assets, notoriously related to the so-called "pre-salt", available to the international market. Regulatory frameworks surrounding the oil sector established during Lula's time in office were removed.

The details and villainy committed in the processes against Lula will be addressed in a separate work. For the purposes of this book, it is important to highlight the perverse manipulation of processes and laws against Lula, to achieve political and geopolitical results that could not have been obtained by traditional means. For this reason and given the relevance of the case, we assert that currently, former President Lula's case represents one of the greatest demonstrations of lawfare.

In conclusion
A point of departure

Through this work we are establishing the basis for a *theory* regarding the phenomenon of lawfare. We do not assert the *truth* on the subject, but rather formulate our own authentic, and to a great extent, previously unpublished vision of a central concern for contemporary constitutional democracies.

Lawfare – from a theoretical and practical perspective – presents great difficulties. To begin with, there is the plurality of knowledge required to understand and absorb it. Anyone limiting themselves to a merely dogmatic and legal approach to the phenomenon will surely not grasp it in its theoretical and practical terms.

Throughout this work we believe we have made it sufficiently clear that lawfare is a serious issue and for this reason deserves significant and thorough attention. Simplifying it as a mere rhetorical instrument, even with the best of intentions, is as damaging as the scepticism or prejudice with which some view it.

At this precise moment, countless people, on every continent, are victims of a diffuse, undeclared, but nonetheless deadly war. We hope that this book will contribute to unveiling the grim state of affairs, in which, in the name of "fighting" corruption, terrorism and other "worthy" causes, the destruction of the law and rights takes place.

There is even more to be said in further editions of this book, in which we will elaborate upon our reflection on lawfare. We hope that our readers will join us on this unique and challenging journey.

Bibliographic references

AGACCI, Matheus. "O overcharging no processo penal brasileiro". Retrieved from: www.migalhas.com.br/dePeso/16,MI311225,31047-+overcharging+no+process o+penal+brasileiro. Page visited 3 September 2019.

AGAMBEN, Giorgio. *Estado de exceção*, 2nd ed. São Paulo: Boitempo, 2004.

ANDRADE NETO, João. "Participante ou observador? Uma escolha entre duas perspectivas metodológicas de estudo e aplicação do Direito". *Revista Direito GV*, vol. 12, no. 3, 2016.

BADARÓ, Gustavo Henrique. *Processo penal*, 4th ed. São Paulo: Revista dos Tribunais, 2016.

BANDEIRA DE MELLO,Celso Antônio. *Curso de Direito Administrativo*, 34th ed. São Paulo: Malheiros, 2019.

BASILIEN-GAINCHE, Marie-Laure. *État de droit et états d'exception:* une conception de l'état. Paris: PUF, 2013.

BEAUFRE, André. *Introduction a la stratégie*. Paris: Librairie Armand Colin, 1963.

BIELSA, Rafael; PERETTI, Pedro. *Lawfare*: guerra judicial-mediática. Buenos Aires: Ariel, 2019.

BOBBIO, Norberto; MATTEUCCI, Nicola; PASQUINO, Gianfranco (Eds.). *Dicionário de política*, 13th ed. vol. 1. Brasília: Editora Universidade de Brasília, 2010.

BURROWS, Megan. "Information warfare: What and how?" Retrieved from: www .cs.cmu.edu/~burnsm/InfoWarfare.html. Page visited 3 September 2019.

CARLSON, John; YEOMANS, Neville. "Whither goeth the law: Humanity or barbarity". *In*: SMITH, Margareth; CROSSLEY, David (Eds.), *The way out*: Radical alternatives in Australia. Melbourne: Lansdowne Press, 1975. Retrieved from: www.laceweb.org.au/whi.htm. Page visited 3 September 2019.

CARRIÓ, Genaro. *Notas sobre derecho y lenguaje*, 3rd ed. Buenos Aires: Abeledo-Perrot, 1986.

CARTER, Phillip. "Legal combat: Are enemies waging war in our courts?" Retrieved from: https://slate.com/news-and-politics/2005/04/legal-combat.html. Page visited 3 September 2019.

CARY, Rob. *Not guilty*: The unlawful prosecution of U.S. Senator Ted Stevens. Washington: Thomson Reuters, 2014.

CLAUSEWITZ, Carl von. *Da guerra*, 3rd ed. São Paulo: Martins Fontes, 2014.

COHEN, Paul H.; PAPALASKARIS, Angela M. *International corruption*, 2nd ed. London: Sweet & Maxwell, 2018.

COMAROFF, John L. "Colonialism, culture, and the law: A foreword". *Law & Social Inquiry*, vol. 26, no. 2, pp. 305–314, 2006.

COMAROFF, John L.; COMAROFF, Jean. "Law and disorder in postcolony". *Social Anthropology/Anthropologie Sociale*, vol. 15, no. 2, pp. 133–152, 2007.

COOKE, Nicole A. *Fake news and alternative facts: Information literacy in post-truth era*. Chicago: LA Editions, 2018.

CROSS, Frank. "Judicial independence". *In*: WHITTINGTON, Keith E.; KELEMEN, Daniel R.; CALDEIRA, Gregory A. (Eds.). *The Oxford handbook of law and politics*. Oxford: Oxford University Press, 2008, p. 559.

DAUGHERTY, William E. *A psychological warfare casebook*. Baltimore: John Hopkins Press, 1958.

DESPORTES, Vincent. "La stratégie en theories". *Politique Étrangère*, 2014/2, pp. 165–178, 2014.

DUNLAP JR, CHARLES J. "Does lawfare need an apologia?" *Case Western Reserve Journal of International Law*, vol. 43, no. 2, 2010.

DUNLAP JR, CHARLES J. "Law and military interventions: Preserving humanitarian values in 21st century conflicts". Working Paper. Cambridge, MA: Harvard University, John F. Kennedy School of Government, 2001. Retrieved from: https://scholarship.law.duke.edu/faculty_scholarship/3500/. Page visited 3 September 2019.

DUNLAP JR, CHARLES J. "Lawfare today: A perspective". *Yale Journal of International Affairs*, Winter 2008, pp. 146–154.

FENWICH, Helen; PHILLIPSON, Gavin. *Media freedom under the Human Rights Act*. New York: Oxford University Press, 2006.

FERES JÚNIOR, João; SASSARA, Luna de Oliveira. "Corrupção, escândalos e a cobertura midiática da política". *Novos Estudos CEBRAP*, vol. 35, no. 2, pp. 205–225, 2016.

FERNANDES, António Horta. *O Homo estrategicus ou a ilusão de uma razão estratégica?* Lisbon: Edições Cosmos, 1998.

FERRAJOLI, Luigi. *A democracia através dos direitos*: o constitucionalismo garantista como modelo teórico e como projeto político. São Paulo: Revista dos Tribunais, 2015.

FERRAJOLI, Luigi. *Razones jurídicas del pacifismo*. Madrid: Editorial Trotta, 2004.

FRAGOSO, Rodrigo. "Overcharging: A prática de exagerar nas acusações". Retrieved from: www.infomoney.com.br/colunistas/crimes-financeiros/over charging-a-pratica-de-exagerar-nas-acusacoes/. Page visited 3 September 2019.

FRANCISCO. "Discurso del Santo Padre Franscisco en la Cumbre de Jueces Panamericanos sobre derechos sociales y doctrina fransciscana". Retrieved from: http://w2.vatican.va/content/francesco/es/speeches/2019/june/documents/papa-fran cesco_20190604_giudici-panamericani.html?fbclid=IwAR1u0b1OogQqzfCylPYb Sr13S-_mz_clj4Jtc DjMEbsDOTpFzs_3jFLkcDY. Page visited 3 September 2019.

GALULA, David. *Counterinsurgency warfare: Theory and practice*. London: Praeger Security International, 2006.

GLOPPEN, Siri. "Conceptualizing lawfare". Retrieved from: www.academia.ed
u/35608212/Conceptualizing_Lawfare_A_Typology_and_Theoretical_Fra
mwork. Page visited 3 September 2019.

GORDON, Neve. "Human rights as a security threat: Lawfare and the campaign
against human rights NGOs". *Law & Society Review*, vol. 48, no. 2, pp. 311–344,
2014.

GOUPY, Marie. *L'état d'exception ou l'impussaince autoritaire de l'état à l'époque
du libéralisme*. Paris: CNRS Éditions, 2016.

GRAY, Colin S. *Theory of strategy*. Oxford: Oxford University Press, 2018.

HANDMAKER, J.D. "Researching legal mobilisation and lawfare". *ISS Working
Papers – General Series*, no. 641. Retrieved from: http://hdl.handle.net/1765
/115129. Page visited 3 September 2019.

HART, Herbert L.A. *O conceito de Direito*, 5th ed. Lisbon: Fundação Calouste
Gulbenkian, 2007.

HOBBES, Thomas. *Leviatã*, 3rd ed. São Paulo: Martins Fontes, 2014.

HOLEINDRE, Jean-Vincent. "La pensée stratégique à l'épreuve de la guerre totale.
De Clausewitz à Liddell Hart". *Éthique, politique, religions*, no. 10, pp. 49–65,
2017.

HORTON, Scott. "The dangers of lawfare". *Case Western Reserve Journal of
International Law*, vol. 43, pp. 163–179, 2010.

HOUNET, Yazid ben. "Lawfare: pourquoi il faut prendre Jean-Luc Mélenchon au
sérieux". Retrieved from: www.liberation.fr/debats/2019/09/24/lawfare-pourqu
oi-il-faut-prendre-jean-luc-melenchon-au-serieux_1753110. Page visited 24
September 2019.

HUGHES, David. "What does lawfare mean?" *Fordham International Law Journal*,
no. 40, pp. 1–40, 2016.

ISRAËL, Liora. *L'arme du droit*. Paris: Presses de Sciences Po, 2009.

JANOT, Rodrigo. *Nada menos que tudo*: bastidores da operação que colocou o
sistema político em xeque. São Paulo: Planeta, 2019.

JOWETT, Garth S.; O'DONNELL, Victoria. *Propaganda and persuasion*, 5th ed.
Los Angeles: SAGE Publications, 2012.

KELSEN, Hans. *A paz pelo direito*. São Paulo: WMF Martins fontes, 2011.

KENNEDY, David. *Of war and war*. Princeton: Princeton University Press, 2006.

KIRCHHEIMER, Otto. *Political justice:* The use of legal procedure for political
ends. Princeton: Princeton University Press, 1961.

KITTRIE, Orde F. *Lawfare*: Law as a weapon of war. Oxford: Oxford University
Press, 2016.

KNIGHTLEY, Phillip. *The first casualty*: From the Crimea to Vietnam: The war
correspondent as hero, propagandist, and myth maker. New York: Harcourt,
Brace Jovanovich, 1975.

KOEHLER, Mike. "The facade of FCPA enforcement". *Georgetown Journal of
International Law*, vol. 41, no. 4, pp. 907–1009, 2010.

KORYBKO, Andrew. *Guerras Híbridas*: das revoluções coloridas aos golpes. São
Paulo: Expressão Popular, 2018.

LACOSTE, Yes. *A geografia*: isso serve, em primeiro lugar, para fazer a guerra, 19th
ed. Campinas: Papirus, 2012.

LE ROUX, Michelle; DAVIS, Dennis. *Lawfare*: Judging politics in South Africa. Johannesburg: Jonathan Ball Publishers, 2019.

LIANG, Qiao; XIANGSUI, Wang. *Unrestricted warfare*. Beijing: PLA Literature and Arts Publishing House, 1999.

LIBICKI, Martin C. *What is information warfare?* Washington: National Defense University, 1995.

LIPPKE, Richard L. *The ethics of plea bargaining*. Oxford: Oxford University Press, 2011.

LUBAN, David J.; O'SULLIVAN, Julie R.; STEWART, David P.; JAIN, Neha. *International and transnational criminal law*. New York: Wolters Kluwer, 2019.

MACDONALD, Scot. *Propaganda and information warfare in the twenty-first century*: Altered images and deception operations. London: Routledge, 2007.

MARAVALL, José María. "Rule of Law as a political weapon". *In*: MARAVALL, José María; PRZEWORSKI, Adam (Eds.), *Democracy and the Rule of Law*. Cambridge: Cambridge University Press, 2003.

MARTINS, Raúl François *Acerca do conceito de estratégia*. Lisbon: IDN, 1984, p. 104.

NOONE, Gregory P. "Lawfare or strategic communications". *Case Western Reserve Journal of International Law*, vol. 43, pp. 73–85, 2010.

NOVAES, Adauto (Coord.). *Ética*. São Paulo: Companhia Das Letras, 2007.

ORWELL, George. *1984*. Nova Iorque: Harcourt, 1977.

PAYE, Jean-Claude. *La fin de l'état de droit*: la lutte antiterroriste, de l'état d'exception à la dictadure. Paris: La Dispute, 2004.

POWELL, Sidney. *Licensed to lie:* Exposing corruption in the Department of Justice. Dallas: Brown Books, 2014.

RECHSTEINER, Beat Walter. *Direito internacional privado: Teoria e prática*, 18th ed. São Paulo: Editora Saraiva, 2016.

ROBERTSON, Geoffrey; NICOL, Andrew. *Media law*. 5th ed. Thomson: Sweet & Maxwell, 2007.

SAINT-BONNET, François. "L'état d'exception et la qualification juridique". *Cahiers de la recherche sur les droits fondamentaux*, no. 6, pp. 29–38, 2008.

SAINT-PIERRE, Héctor Luis; VITELLI, Marina Gisela (Eds.). *Dicionário de segurança e defesa*. São Paulo: Editora Unesp, Imprensa Oficial do Estado de São Paulo, 2018.

SERRANO, Pedro Estevam Alves Pinto. *Autoritarismo e golpes na América Latina*: breve ensaio sobre jurisdição e exceção. São Paulo: Alameda, 2016.

SCHAUER, Frederick. "Exceptions". *The University of Chicago Law Review*, Chicago, vol. 58, no. 3, pp. 871–899, 1991.

SCHMITT, Carl. *La notion de politique*. Paris: Flammarion, 1992.

SCHMITT, Carl. *Political theology*: Four chapters on the concept of sovereignty. Chicago: University of Chicago Press, 2005.

SPALDING, Andrew Brady. "Unwitting sanctions: Understanding anti-bribery legislation as economic sanctions against emerging markets". *Florida Law Review*, pp. 351–427, 2009.

STRECK, Lenio Luiz. *Verdade e consenso*: constituição, hermenêutica e teorias discursivas, 6th ed. São Paulo: Saraiva, 2017.

TIEFENBRUN, Susan. "Semiotic definition of lawfare". *Case Western Reserve Journal of International Law*, vol. 43, pp. 29–60, 2010.

TZU, Sun. *A arte da guerra*, 24th ed. São Paulo: Record, 2001.

VALIM, Rafael. *A subvenção no Direito Administrativo brasileiro*. São Paulo: Editora Contracorrente, 2015.

VALIM, Rafael. *O princípio da segurança jurídica no Direito Administrativo brasileiro*. São Paulo: Malheiros, 2010.

VALIM, Rafael; COLANTUONO, Pablo Ángel Gutiérrez. *Estado de exceção. a forma jurídica do neoliberalismo*. São Paulo: Editora Contracorrente, 2017.

VALIM, Rafael; COLANTUONO, Pablo Ángel Gutiérrez. "O enfrentamento da corrupção nos limites do Estado de Direito". *In*: ZANIN MARTINS, Cristiano; ZANIN MARTINS, Valeska Teixeira; VALIM, Rafael (Eds.), *O Caso Lula*: a luta pela afirmação dos direitos fundamentais no Brasil. São Paulo: Editora Contracorrente, 2017.

WEISSMAN, Andrew; SMITH, Alixandra. *Restoring balance, proposed amendments to Foreign Corrupt Practices Act. U.S.* Chamber Institute for Legal Reform. The FCPA Blog, 2011. Retrieved from: www.fcpablog.com/blog2011/4/8/jj-joinew-new-top-ten.html. Page visited 3 September 2019.

WERNER, Wouter G. "The curious career of lawfare". *Case Western Reserve Journal of International Law*, no. 43–2, pp. 61–72, 2010.

ZAFFARONI, E. Raúl. *O inimigo no Direito Penal*, 2nd ed. Rio de Janeiro: Revan, 2007.

Index

Printed in the United States
by Baker & Taylor Publisher Services

Printed in the United States
by Baker & Taylor Publisher Services